Books by Wright Morris

Plains Song

Plains Song

FOR FEMALE VOICES

A NOVEL BY

Wright Morris

NONPAREIL
BOOKS

David R. Godine, Publisher

BOSTON

This is a Nonpareil Book
published in 1991 by
David R. Godine, Publisher, Inc.
Horticultural Hall
300 Massachusetts Avenue
Boston, Massachusetts 02115

First published in 1980 by Harper & Row Publishers.

Library of Congress Cataloging in Publication Data
Morris, Wright, 1910–
Plains song for female voices / Wright Morris.
p.   cm.
ISBN 0-87923-835-6
I. Title.
PS3525.07475P5 1991
813'.52—dc20   89-46184   CIP

FIRST PRINTING
Manufactured in the United States of America

Plains Song

It is a curse in this family that the women bear only daughters, if anything at all.

"Let her nap," said a voice. "She needs her nap."

Cora does not need a nap, but she welcomes silence. Is the past a story we are persuaded to believe, in the teeth of the life we endure in the present? Even Cora Atkins, whose life is over? Her mind is sealed, like a tomb, but her eyes are open. The humiliations of age have won from her one concession: the nightcap she wears to conceal her baldness. Silken wisps of hair loop over the pulleys of her ears, the parts of her body that have never stopped growing, but the dome of her head is smooth as a gourd. Chairs have been brought in for the visitors to sit on, but none resemble the woman propped up in the bed. Age has eliminated the frills of individual distinction. She looks old, as her grandchildren look young. She was never spry, comforting, or twinkling, and the young are reluctant to call her Grandma to her face. Nor do they raise their faces to her to be kissed. Not that she is cold, unloving, or insensible. She is implacable. Her talon-like hands lie before her, the right placed on the left, a scar blue as gun metal between the first and second knuckle, a seam on the flesh. How did she acquire it? It is said a horse bit her. For a farmer's wife that is not unusual. She had stood in the doctor's office, near the glare at the window where he had looked at her hand with the torn flesh, the knuckle bone exposed. "What happened?" he had asked. She had been speechless. Tobacco juice oozing at the corner of his mouth, her husband, Emerson, had said, "Horse bit her." She had been both relieved and appalled. But she preferred it to admitting she had bitten herself.

Would it have been better if she had stayed with her father, a gentle man with a cracked, pleading voice? She sees him looming above her, one long arm stretched to the top shelf behind the counter, where a can, with peaches on the label, tilts forward to fall into the hammock of his apron. Before placing it right side up on the counter, he will give the lid a swipe with a wad of the apron. He was reluctant to sell it. He stocked only the best, and hated to sell his stock. Nothing equaled his pleasure, every morning, in sprinkling the floor with sawdust, then sweeping it up. He liked to clean up, to wash up, to fix up. He wore a cap made of a folded Boston newspaper, and licked his fingers after ladling the butter. She saw him best when he leaned forward, his glasses low on his nose, to read the weight on the scales.

A voice in the room says, "She needs her sleep."

What Cora sees, now that her eyes are lidded, is the father slicing cheese, pausing to pick up the crumbs with his moistened finger. The smell of brine in the pickle barrel puckers her lips. But she no longer sees things too clearly. The glass of memory ripples, or is smoked and darkened like isinglass. Her father had written to a brother, who had settled in Ohio, that his daughter was now of marriageable age. A young woman who was taller and stronger than most would surely be appreciated where women were lacking. She was also experienced as a seamstress, and could keep accounts.

It had been unthinkable, and Cora did not think it, that she would go against her father's wishes. If it so happened that marriage did not materialize, that disaster would be faced, but one did not think about it. A spinster aunt of Cora's had spent her entire life traveling from one relation to another, helping with the chores, the sickness, the new babies. She had had the labor and care of children, but none of the insurance for old age. That winter Cora had been twenty, lean rather than thin, with what she had heard described as an English complexion. Her eyes were prominent in her angular face. A portrait taken in Salem is characteristically solemn. She was somewhat fleshier than she would ever be again, but the man who took her arm would find it firm and spare as a rail. Perhaps her height made her unsure of her footing: she walked stiffly, with her elbows lifted. This had the effect of fencing her off from smaller, friendlier people. Kin of her mother, with five marriageable daughters, took her with them on their way to Wisconsin, where it was said that able-bodied girls, on the plump side, would soon find takers.

In matters of a religious nature, Cora was more into depth of feeling than she was the fine points of dogma. Feeling gave her the truth of the matter, quite beyond the resources of argument. She never lacked for self-knowledge in the matter of vanity. Mirrors impressed her as suspect by nature in the way they presented a graven image. She keenly and truly felt the deception of her reflected glance. Being a practical woman she did not forgo mirrors, but they revealed so little of a person so large she was kept in ignorance. She did her hair in two braids, parted at the rear then curved about her head to meet at the crown, but at twenty years of age she could not tell you what prospect this offered from the rear. She had never held a mirror in such a manner that she might see. A good thing, perhaps, since the wide part showed too much of her bone-white scalp, and the exposure of neck revealed the knobby vertebrae of the spine like a clenched fist. Neither had she (since a child) gazed with open eyes on what the Lord had created below her neck. Long underwear concealed it most of the year, with the assistance of lamplight and early darkness, and she would have sooner spied on her father than glanced at the mirror to see her own nude body. Was that in modesty or repugnance? She needed no mirror to be fully aware that her clothes hung on her body as if from a hanger, and no seamstress would refer to her chest as a bust. Her able-bodied second cousins were well endowed in this department, but slow-witted and lazy. Their mother turned to Cora when she wanted something done. "God pity the men you marry!" she would say too often, but there was never any doubt that men would. From their father she had the disturbing assurance that ignorant and inexperienced young men might overlook her, but a man with kids to raise, who had lost a wife, would see in her the virtues of a good hired hand. They left her with her Uncle Myron, a hotel and stable owner, who did most of his business with travelers from the east, but there were occasionally men from the west who returned to replenish their supplies of horses and livestock, hardware and software, beans and bacon, flour and lard, seed grain, tobacco, and perhaps a wife.

Just the previous fall Emerson Atkins had gone west with his brother, Orion, to homestead government land on the great plains. The rich land along the Platte River had been settled, but just north of the Elkhorn, in Madison County, the brothers settled a claim and spent the season planting trees for shade and shelter. A cautious, some would say suspicious man, Emerson thought it better to return to Ohio for supplies than deal with the sharks at the Missouri crossings.

Emerson—he had the name from a pastor, admired by his mother—had the stolid heavy-bottomed figure and slow deliberate movements of a man of forty. His brother, Orion, looked half his age, but at twenty-five was just two years his junior. The spring Emerson met Cora he was clean-shaven, but the previous winter he had been bearded. His hair was brown, but one saw little of it since he took most of his meals with his hat on. A broom straw or long stem of grass was usually wagging at the front of his mouth. He had found it cheaper to chew tobacco than smoke it, so he chewed it. As a rule he was polite but ill at ease with young women, whom he knew to have cagey designs on men. He differed from the blonder, friendlier Orion, however, in not considering himself a "catch." He gave the impression that he was prudent and assured, but not vain. Any decision at all—such as what to eat on the dinner menu—prompted Emerson into periods of brooding but did not make him impatient. Impatient waitresses could walk away, as they usually did, or wait for him to reach a decision. Cora distinguished herself by waiting. Glancing up to see who it was, it was her that he saw. In the course of a week he removed his hat before taking his seat at the table. Although inexperienced, Cora knew men from boys. The slow, almost drawling speech of Emerson had the effect of putting her at her ease. His humor was drier than any she had heard; even his eyes betrayed no twinkle. A watch that he wound with a key occupied his attention after eating, the hinged lid of the case reflecting the lamplight on the room's pressed-tin ceiling. From her uncle she learned that his name was Emerson, which she thought appropriate.

It flatters a man to possess a woman who attracts the envious glances of other men, with her exceptional carriage or well-turned ankles, but a subtler admiration may be aroused if the woman is lacking in such attractions. A plain woman may well have been chosen for her character, or womanly nature, or because the poor devil actually loved her. In any case, the man's motives might have been of a higher rather than a lower order. Such a woman gets a second, appraising look to determine what it is the man sees in her. Such a man is judged as subtly superior to the attractions that contribute little to a sound marriage, the establishment of a home, and the proper rearing of a family. It reassures those men who have made a similar decision, and is the envy of those who have acted less wisely.

A young woman six feet tall, with an English complexion, is not accurately described as plain. Cora's solemn face, her sober gaze, brought to most men's minds some image of a schoolmarm, and this seemed appropriate to her height. She wore practical blouses, sateen cuffs to protect the sleeves, and in the way of ornament a small gold pin at the collar. The under garments appropriate to all women gave her hips a roundness that was deceptive, but nothing could have been further from her purpose. What could a woman do if modest attire merely enhanced what she meant to conceal? The question is rhetorical: so far as is known, she never asked it. She saw enough of Emerson Atkins in his two-week stay—he extended it a week because of the weather—to grow more or less accustomed to his "joshing" and listen with interest to his comments. She heard the name Ryan innumerable times before she grasped that he meant to say O-rion, the name of his younger brother. His manner of speech was droll, as well as slurred, and led her to be a more attentive listener. Telling a story, for example, he said "s'i," for "says I," or "s'ee," for "says he," which she found highly irregular and often confusing. She managed to learn that 'Rion had been left on the farm, where he was building a house and putting in the first crop. There was neither pride nor affection in his voice, but that might have been due to his manner. Each brother had his own piece of land, but they planned to pool their resources and farm it together. That way the equipment to handle one farm would farm two. Together they would build separate homes, then lead separate lives. 'Rion understood that. Being brothers, they had seen enough of each other growing up.

Nor did it seem unusual to Cora that a man like Emerson would confide in a stranger. He was alone. He had much of the day to sit around and talk. As the only child of a widowed father, Cora was long accustomed to the talk of men. Her father had talked cheese, and quality canned goods, which he preferred to keep rather than sell. Emerson Atkins was a farmer. He talked knowledgeably of horses, Holstein cows, compared Plymouth Rocks to Leghorns, and pigs to hogs. In a new country, like it was, he saw a future in dairy products and hogs.

From her Uncle Myron's wife, a woman both plain and worn, and for that reason more sympathetic to Cora, she learned that Mr. Atkins had inquired if she might be open to an offer of marriage. Was she flabbergasted? So her uncle reported in a letter to her father. "Dear Cora is flabbergasted," he wrote, "by the prospect of life west of the Missouri . . .," an outright falsehood since it had not crossed her mind to ask or to wonder what his farm might be west of. Unmentioned in the letter, but implicit, was the fact that if Emerson left without her, he would hardly return such a distance for her. Mr. Atkins possessed, in Myron's opinion, the experience and capital to make a good marriage. He evinced no bad habits. To speak frankly—and he went on to do it—Cora was no prize, although her attainments were considerably beyond the ordinary. She was excellent at figures. As a wife she would be both sensible and frugal. The uncle would recommend that Cora accept Mr. Atkins, if she felt no aversion toward him, but he would not press her in this decision since he judged her to be of an independent cast of mind, a young woman who could act and think for herself.

If a distinction might be made, Cora felt more dazed than flabbergasted. She had assumed she would have time to acquaint herself with suitors, or would feel toward one of them a strong attraction. Nor had she dreamed that she would become a bride without an engagement. On the other hand, she certainly felt no aversion, if one excepted his habit of chewing and spitting tobacco. Before he spat, his lips puckered like a fat hen's bottom; afterward he gave them a twist, between his thumb and forefinger, to clean them. It was something that custom would accustom a woman to. A young seamstress from Buffalo, with a child but no husband, confided to Cora that a long engagement might deprive a woman of what little pleasure a marriage offered. She seemed willing to explain herself, if encouraged, but Cora felt it a breach of the marriage vows to openly discuss such a question. First of all, she knew nothing. What she would come to learn was for her alone to know.

A further word from Mr. Atkins—hardly a stratagem; it seemed unlikely his mind worked in such a manner—admitted that the suddenness of his proposal might be unfair to Miss Cora, as he called her, and suggested that she might postpone her decision for the two or three weeks he would be on the road. In Omaha he would find her considered answer. If it was yes, he would wait and she would come on by train to join him. This concession pleased Cora and surely testified to Mr. Atkins's good sense and honorable intent. At the same time it assured Cora that such a postponement was not advisable. What better time to enlarge her knowledge and understanding of her husband than a leisurely trip across the woodlands and prairies in the spring of the year? Not soon again—the young seamstress assured her—would she spend idle days in the seat of a buggy, and eat meals prepared by others. For Cora, more fortunate than most women, this trip would constitute her honeymoon, the pause between her life such as it had once been and the endless chores of a farmer's wife.

Chores held no terrors for Cora—quite the contrary, something as explicit as chores were welcome—but implicit in the words of the ceremony were thoughts that clouded her mind long after they were spoken. The marriage itself, in the house of her uncle, rooms having been added to accommodate his growing family, was attended by members of the pastor's family. A man of strong religious feeling, he carried the faith to his flock by horseback. Some of what he said confused her, but his emotion sealed her vows. She might, and she would, suffer from what was understood to be bondage, but she would never question that it had been sanctioned by God.

From her window the following morning, she observed her husband bargaining with a man to drive the wagon loaded with supplies and tend to the team. Cora raised the window to remind him that she was not lacking experience with horses. The young man was not pleased to lose the offer of a job, but he smiled with admiration at Cora. Never before had she felt so keenly the pleasurable flush of her own importance. Emerson's sober gaze seemed more respectful.

"You'll feel it in the back," he said to her later, and put a hand to that area where she would feel it, a liberty, surely, but with no more pressure than a waiter guiding her to a table. They had not exchanged glances. From the first they had done their talking with their eyes averted, as if collecting their thoughts.

After the first day's drive she felt it more in the shoulders, but she knew that the back would come later. She found it a relief to walk beside the buggy where the going was slow, her skirts sweeping the grass. The Illinois prairie was like nothing she had seen, but in harmony with much that she had imagined. Having lived near the sea, she was familiar with boundless horizons. Calling his name aloud, hearing him answer, reconciled her to its strangeness. He was Emerson. He pronounced the word "Cora" as he did "caw." In the fall, on his trip east, Emerson had experienced troublesome clouds of mosquitoes and insects, but in early April they had few complaints but the muscular soreness and the morning chill. She slept on a place he had prepared in the wagon, he slept beneath. This seemed to her an example of the wisdom she might expect from her husband. It was not the time or place, weary and physically sore, for whatever it was she had been led to expect. The ground was soggy and thawing, but they were spared heavy rains. Between the pages of a book of ladies' fashions Cora pressed flowers for which she lacked names. Was this what she would find where they were going? Emerson seemed to be of two opinions. The soil had more sand in it. The prevailing wind blew from the southwest. Most people noticed the sparseness of trees, but that would change as more were planted. Hundreds had been planted. In a few years they would give cool shade. In a six-hour period enough rain had fallen to fill a milk pail to overflowing. It was easier to wait and see what happened than to say what might.

She came to see that her husband was a man of few words, and one unvarying mood. His voice might be raised, in handling the horses, but she saw no rise in his temper. When he walked beside the wagon, to stretch his legs, he had the lumbering gait, the downcast eyes, of a horse at ease in the harness. His nature was like that of good livestock. Accustomed to pauses, he would sometimes sit with the reins in his hands, letting the team wander. From what he told her, Orion was different. He liked to hunt, and tinker with machinery. In some ways he bewildered Emerson, but only if he saw too much of him. As soon as it could be managed he would have his own place.

Cora welcomed demands of a useful nature, such as the chores of a household, the mending of clothes, the care and hoarding of limited resources, but she had given little thought to the breeding of children. They would come. It was for this he had taken a wife. Whatever Emerson's feelings or thoughts in such matters, they were like hers in that he kept them to himself. This shared characteristic made for repose, whether they stopped to rest the horses or prepare for the night, but what was not shared in this unspoken manner seemed to strain the efforts of speech. Cora could frame the thought, she could choose the words, but his reposeful silence made her reluctant to speak. She looked forward to Burlington, a Mississippi River crossing, where they would stay in an inn, take baths, and Emerson would shave. In the scrub of his beard his face seemed to lack features. His eyes, creased by the wind and the light, were gray as gooseberries, and showed no whites. He seemed startled by her speech, replying, "How's 'at?" in a way that she found distracting. That would change when they were free of the creak of the wagon, and the open air she found intimidating. Her voice might crack, uncertain of its volume or pitch. In Burlington, after a heavy meal, she put herself to bed. He came back from his bath smelling of soap, his face nicked by the razor, his hair up wild from his scrubbed scalp, his thick body tight in a suit of oatmeal-colored flannel. For some time, as if alone, he sat on the edge of the bed rubbing his scalp. His hair needed cutting: his head, seen from the back, was like that of a just plucked chicken. Nor was he in a hurry. Her heart pounded as he stooped to trim his nails. The words of the seamstress came to her with such force that she saw him as an utter stranger. Before he puffed the lamp out and rolled toward her, the bed creaking like the body of the wagon, her dismay had given way to a dread that paralyzed her will. When he moved on her, his groping hands confusing the sheet with her nightgown, she had already put her clenched fist into her mouth and stared sightlessly at the ceiling. What did she experience? It might be likened to an operation without the anesthesia. Horror exceeded horror. The time required by her assailant to do what must be done left her in shock. In the dawn light she found that she had bitten through the flesh of her hand, exposing the bone. Emerson's bafflement moved him to speech. Aloud he asked how such a thing might have happened. Unable to grasp it, he seemed to doubt what it was he saw. He was able to escort her to the lobby, however, and inquire where they might find a doctor. One block down the street, over a pharmacy, his name shadowed on the half-drawn blind at the window, Dr. Talbot's office was blue with cigar smoke, through which Cora saw the skeleton suspended in the corner. To see Cora's wound clearly, he raised the blind at the window.

"How did this happen?" he asked her, but she had been speechless. He had turned to Emerson, whose lips were puckered to hold in his chew. He looked about for a spittoon, saw one near the desk, lowered his head to relieve himself, then said, "Horse bit her."

With Emerson Dr. Talbot exchanged a glance of understanding. He advised her to be more cautious with horses, and soak the hand, twice a day, in hot water to which Epsom salts had been added. This puzzled and interested Emerson, familiar with the use of salts for other discomforts. The two men discussed horses and farming while the doctor cleaned the wound with alcohol. They then returned to the hotel, where Emerson had his breakfast in the restaurant off the lobby while Cora sat in the bedroom, soaking her hand in hot water. The pain seemed to settle her disordered emotions. Emerson's shameless falsehood had appalled her, but she did not take it as a personal betrayal. He was a man, and spoke this way to other men. As other women had hinted, the time would come when her eyes would be opened and she would be tested. In her soul she knew that one life had ended, and another begun.

Later she removed the bloodied sheet from the bed and wore it under her skirts when Emerson came for her, her blood feverish with emotions that both pleased and shamed her. His offer to help her to the seat of the buggy she declined, managing by herself, gripping the reins in the manner of a woman familiar with the bite of a horse.

While Emerson had been in Ohio, acquiring supplies and a wife, Orion and a part-time hired hand had built a two-room structure with a gabled roof, a loft in the east end of the gable, it being the custom among settlers who could afford it to build a small, temporary dwelling while constructing the main house. Orion being the one with an eye for the ladies, it had never crossed his mind his brother would return with a wife. This woman with the bandaged hand and the somber expression (two inches taller than Orion before she put her shoes on), the morning she arrived, her bag still unpacked, her hand in a sling improvised from a flour sack, cleaned out the mess he had made during the winter and rearranged the house to her liking. To Orion's offer of help (Emerson had been silent, as if this had been determined beforehand) she replied that when she couldn't take care of a house she would not be moving into it. These words were not spoken rudely, but in the interests of clarification. With the bed occupied by the newlyweds, a place was found for Orion behind the new range, where it was close but snug. Although it was Cora's work, being part of her domain, Orion was allowed to shake down the ashes and start up a new cob fire in the morning—it started with a whoosh, when sprinkled with coal oil—since it seemed rude for her to do it with him lying on the floor behind it. It was Emerson's pleasure to fill the pails at the pump and return them to the porch without spilling. Orion could not seem to do that, the length of his legs, or his arms, causing them to sway in such a manner they splashed. Framed in the door (where he was out of her way), Orion would wait to be called to the table, where he would eat with his eyes on his food rather than lift them and gaze at Cora. From the back side, her arms lifted, she reminded him of a witch. What did he know of witches? He had seen them pasted on schoolhouse windows. Feeling his eyes on her back, she had said, "Have you nothing to do but sit and stare like a calf?" Her voice was not shrill, but it was penetrating. Gripped in her good hand, as she spoke to him, she held the nickel-plated wire-handled plate lifter. He

18

stopped staring at her. He spied on her, of course, with quick furtive glances, but what she saw in his face gave her little reason to scowl at him. He was merely dumfounded, an emotion known to her personally.

Orion was almost blond, open-mouthed in a somewhat loutish, adenoidal manner, but he was more responsive than Emerson and not indifferent to a show of feeling. It pleased Cora to note the change in his expression. The calf-like open-mouthed bafflement had changed to ill-concealed admiration. She was indeed a strange beanpole of a woman, but he accepted her as a remarkable wife.

There are women who like to work but do not know how, and women who hate work who push themselves to exhaustion, hardly knowing and never learning that work, in itself, is gratifying. That work was never done reassured Cora. She knew how to work, and asked only that she work to an end. Having worked, she had need to look around and see what she had done. Understandably, her hand recovered quickly, shamed to hang idle in the noose from her neck, and the healing of this wound proved to be of untiring interest to Orion. What would lead a horse, or anything else, to bite a *woman's* hand? He differed from Emerson, who had little interest in such misfortunes, even his own. A jack used to raise or lower the level of the house slipped the cog that held it while his hand was beneath it, smashing three fingers. They looked like pulped mash. Cora's face had blanched to see it: she thought she might faint. The only sound from Emerson, after a few muttered curses, was the statement, "I figure I'll lose the two in the middle." He lost the first l..1uckle of the middle finger, but it could have been worse if it had been the first one, or worse yet if it had been the thumb. Orion was not of that metal, and moaned aloud for two nights with the infection and swelling of an ingrown toenail, with another two days wasted while he sat on a stool soaking the foot in a basin. Emerson came and went as if Orion no longer lived in the house.

The building of the new house was delayed by the need to get the first crops in. The hired hand who helped with plowing was full of advice on the subject of farming. He had been an egg candler, in Illinois, but he had to shift to farming in a country so barren they lacked even eggs to candle. He proved to be a good and willing worker during those hours he had nobody to talk to.

A shed was added to the house for him to sleep in, screened at the windows with mosquito netting. The extra space would also shelter a washing machine, and a cream separator shipped from Kansas City. A greater interruption, lasting several weeks, was the piecemeal arrival of the parts of the windmill. Having seen one, Emerson had to have one, although he lacked the live-stock to really use it. When the parts were assembled, he had to admit he had no idea how to put it all together. Nor did the hired hand. A man came from Omaha to supervise the construction, staying over on Sunday to go hunting with Orion. Once the contrap-tion was up, the wheel gleaming like a sunburst, the pump working at night while the rest of them rested, Cora marveled how the farm had done without it. The creak of the wheel at night gave her comfort and assurance. The sight of it in the morning was like a church steeple. It moved and awed her to watch it shift with the wind, as if on orders from on high. Until the trees grew higher, the spinning wheel was the first thing she saw, on returning from Battle Creek, eight miles east of Norfork, the wife of a farmer who had finally become a farmer's wife.

In the spring, mistakes were detected in the work done over the winter. A miscalculation in the tilt of the roof meant that the second-floor windows were level with the floor, but by raising the lower pane the floor could be swept into the open, until they put up the screens. The hired hand was at pains to tell her that, his crooked face straight.

To save the time lost coming in from the fields at noon, Cora would carry a pail of food to Emerson, which he would eat while the team rested. She might find him at the far end of the section, coming toward her so slowly he hardly seemed to move. Above the creak of the harness she would hear the swish of the stiff denim between his thighs. With the horses his manner was courtly: he addressed the mare as "girl," the roan stallion as "boy." The wind brought his voice to her, the clear Gee and Haw as the furrow wavered. The beasts walked with their heads low, the worn patches on their pelts gleaming. In the deep trough of the furrow, the plow blade in the earth, they appeared to be straining to pull Emerson. Until he arrived, looping the reins about one handle, she might be flushed with pleasurable anticipation.

Emerson's great deliberation, his concern for the fly nets, his shuffling about to pull up grass for the team, held Cora's attention as if she were spellbound but at a remove from what she was seeing. His muttered remarks were for the horses, the slap and stroke of his hand caresses. From the pail she had brought him he would take the buttermilk and drink it half down, then give a rumbling belch. Silently he would eat while she stood watching. The dark furrows he had just plowed seemed to please both him and the birds. Orion might encourage Cora to stand close for a moment and talk, while he showed her something turned up by the plow, but neither arrowheads nor bones held interest for Emerson. His pleasure was to cup a handful of the moist loam, letting it sift between his fingers, or smooth it out on his rough palm as if looking for something. It did not please him that Cora took the time to carry food to Orion, on his own section. In reference to Orion, he first called to her attention that a woman in her condition shouldn't overtire herself. His manner was that it was something she might have overlooked if he hadn't brought it up.

Had Cora ever doubted that the nightmare she had survived would result in a child? The logic of it was clear and not to be questioned. The gift of life was holy, and one paid for it dearly. The drama of creation, as she now understood it, a coming together of unearthly forces, was not unlike the brute and blind disorder of her unthinkable experience. So it was meant to be, and so she had found it. Toward Emerson she felt no personal anger, admitting to the necessity of an accomplice. Only in this wise could the mortal body bring forth new life.

The pastor in Battle Creek, learning of her condition, referred to her discomfort as *wages.* She pondered this, but did not fully understand it. Stretched on her back, she watched the mound of her body swell to conceal the iron frame at the foot of the bed. In the hollow at her side Emerson slept soundly, and she was grateful for his indifference. Orion was always up before her to fetch the basket of cobs, build a fire, and fill the air with the astringent smell of coal oil. The whoosh and crackle of the flames, the sound of water dipped from the pail to splash in the wash pan, began a day that Emerson would end by winding the alarm clock on the range hood, the alarm set for five. That it seldom rang did not arouse his comment. It was part of the clock, and required winding, to ensure that the sun would rise in the morning. The first cackling of her pullets, before the first light of dawn, always found Cora awake.

It seemed ordained to her, rather than by chance, as did the sensible progress of the seasons, that as she grew larger and slower, so did the days grow shorter and the work lessen, accommodating itself to her situation. At prescribed periods, on the doctor's recommendation, she got off her feet. Her long, tapering hands, one with the blue-scarred knuckle, rested on her swollen body as if to calm it, or respond to an expected signal. Appraising her wide hips, the doctor assured her that childbirth would give her little trouble. How could he have known that she found that prediction disappointing? Had she endured so much for a birth of little moment? From day to day, however, being with child gave her the satisfaction of work soon to be completed, a harvest to which she could look forward. One day differed so little from another only Sundays held her attention. She liked the prayer and the worship less than she did the singing of the hymns. Although Emerson had observed the Baptist sabbath in Ohio, he had been reared as Methodist, in Zanesville, but no church of that denomination was nearer than Nehigh, an hour's ride in the buggy. Cora had been raised a Unitarian, but she was not a stickler for denominations. She would go to the service closest by, if hymns were sung. She was amazed and troubled to learn, however, that Catholics had established themselves in the county, although owing their allegiance to neither God nor country, but to the Pope. She would have thought about it if more urgent matters had not been on her mind.

Just before Christmas, during their first intense cold spell, Cora suffered from deep drowsiness, with bad headaches which she assumed to be part of her wages, but Dr. Geltmayer threw open the kitchen door to flood the house with icy blasts of air. If she was ill, he said, it was because she lacked air to breathe. The house with its closed windows, its burning range, lacked oxygen. To explain, Dr. Geltmayer lit a stub of candle and covered it with one of Cora's jelly glasses. They were silent as they watched the flame shrink, then sputter out. Emerson's astonishment was boundless. To believe it, he had to see it done over, examining the glass and lighting the candle with his own match. After that occasion he would say to Cora, "The air cold enough for you to breathe it?" Nothing else he had heard, read, or seen brought him so close to a smile.

The fact was, however, that Cora felt so much better she knew she had been short of air for some time. Too much of it, perhaps, hastened to bring on her labor pains. Orion walked the horse and buggy three miles to the farm of Otto Kahler, whose wife was a midwife, and by the time they had returned, Cora was stretched on the rack, as if meant to be broken. Although urged to cry out by Mrs. Kahler, Cora made no sound. Unable to bear the silence, Orion left the house and found Emerson in the storm cave, sorting the sprouting potatoes. The air in the cave was moist and almost warm, fragrant with the smell of the lantern. When he returned to the house the child was howling, but the woman on the bed appeared to be dead. It clarified Orion's first impression that she was a woman of remarkable appearance. She was not dead, but in a place so like it no one but herself might have drawn the distinction. She had lost so much blood that Mrs. Kahler marveled how a body so thin had managed to contain it. From where had it all come? How could it be replaced? Just a few days before, Orion had remarked the fever-like pricks of color in her English complexion, but now her face in the lamplight was like wet plaster. He wondered if any person should come back from where she had been. He was sent out to fetch Emerson, so that the father might see the mother and child together, both of them alive. When shown the wrinkled, howling infant, he commented that she squawked pretty good for a girl.

The little tyke, as Emerson described her, was heavier than most boys Mrs. Kahler had delivered. Given the bottle, she stopped her squalling, like a good child. The strain of the birth had changed Cora's color, and hollowed her cheeks as if teeth were missing. She looked more like Abe Lincoln to Orion than Emerson's wife. What a strange sight it was to see her with the child. Her unbraided hair hung in lank, oily strands, her scalp showing bone white where the hair parted. However strange she looked, she proved to be of one mind about the infant's name. It would be Beulah Madge, the Beulah after the mother of Emerson and Orion, the Madge after the mother of Cora's father. It had been her name that Cora heard the most often as a symbol of womanly attainments. It was to her that Cora owed her high coloring, if not her temperament.

Emerson's comment was that with a name like that a girl would not find it hard to frighten off the boys. A moon-faced child, with light-brown hair that grew forward and down from the crown's bald spot, she had Emerson's small pale eyes, his chubby paw-like hands. Her complexion was that of a smooth Plymouth Rock egg. But if there was so little to remind one of Cora, was that cause for complaint? In line with the facts as seen by Orion, or the few people he spoke to, the girls would do better to take after the father, and the sons, if any, after the mother. In such strange ways, surely, the Lord went about his mysterious work.

Along with the father's moon face, and his comforting figure, Beulah Madge inherited his constitution. Nothing fazed Emerson. Only lack of nourishment disturbed the child. Most infants deprived of their mother's milk were predictably wayward and choleric, subject to rashes and digestive disorders, with a corresponding sourness of breath, temperament, and outlook on life. Not Beulah Madge. The child cried so seldom Cora wondered if a faculty might be missing. In this she differed from Emerson, who took its equable nature for granted. It played with his paw-like calloused hand. When bounced on his knee it hiccuped and giggled. On Cora's insistence, however, it was denied the pleasure of sucking or chewing on his overall buttons. In the taking of food, in the soiling of diapers, she was methodical and tireless. In a wedge-shaped box made from a feed trough, she would lie gurgling and content to stare at the shadows moving on the ceiling. Each time the ashes were shaken, the air in the kitchen danced with dust motes. Cora worried that such air might be too thick to breathe, but not for Beulah Madge. As the cold tapered off, and the windows were opened, letting in the bird songs and the cackle of the hens, Beulah Madge was referred to as Madge. Perhaps Beulah seemed a large label on such a small package. Madge was what her father called her, words of one syllable coming natural to him, this one escaping his mouth with no visible parting of his teeth or loss of tobacco juice. It was not Cora's nature to handle or fondle a child if it would sit by itself. The bald spot on Madge's crown troubled her, but she was reassured that it was temporary, as was her craving for feathers when Cora plucked a chicken, and turned to see the child with a mouthful, like one of the cats. The lightness and flatness of her own body pleased Cora, but she still found it a strain to lift the child to her hip or hold her for burping. Orion assumed this chore, patting her to the tune of nursery songs that irritated Emerson. If it was his intent to yahoo and yodel, would he get on with the building of his own house? The long wintering together, in the unfinished house, had aggravated the way the brothers rubbed one another, Orion leaving the house after breakfast to not return until Emerson had eaten. Cora kept his food in the range warmer, but he would bolt it in silence, then leave the house. Where did he go? On the moonlit nights he walked in the fields with his gun. The sound of it firing exasperated Emerson, certain he would kill himself or somebody more useful. Orion set his traps on the banks of the Elkhorn, where he trapped skunks, muskrats, and rabbits. The skinned bodies of the creatures repelled Cora, and she could seldom bring herself to eat the flesh. Ducks she felt to be different; she heard them honking at night, and welcomed the long-necked, almost legless creatures with their still unruffled feathers concealing their dark, shot-pitted flesh. Orion liked the bird roasted, but Emerson com-

28

plained that swallowed lead pellets remained in the stomach, or worse yet, got into the veins and made these bumps and lumps.

In March the ground was firm enough to move the kitchen range from the temporary house to the new one, the draft up the new chimney so strong it would suck the flame from a wad of corn husks. A porch had been planned for the front of the house, where they might sit on summer evenings, free of the heat off the kitchen, but for the time being the wood was used to construct a platform porch at the back, low to the ground but running the width of the house. It would be deep enough to take the washing machine, with its tubs and pails, and a line to hang laundry in rainy weather. The floor was tilted to drain wash spill and drippings, and the one low step to the yard was no higher than a child could take, when it had to, which might be soon. Inside the house only the living room was plastered, the others ribbed with laths like a corn-crib, looking more like a building that was coming down than one going up. The stairs to the bedrooms, however, were heated like a warming oven by the chimney, so that Cora leaned on it for warmth as she went up and down. Furniture was lacking, and colorful wallpaper, but lace curtains screened the light at two windows, with green blinds at the front on rollers. Who was to look in at them but her chickens? Emerson asked. Two large crates of pullets, all of them Plymouth Rocks with the exception of two confused Rhode Island Red roosters, sat for almost a week at the station in Battle Creek before Emerson got the word to come and get them. For two or three days they cackled all day and half the night. It had been Cora's intention to fence them in (the chickens were her problem, not Emerson's), but they scratched up food for themselves running loose, and she liked the way, hearing her in the morning, they would come clucking to gather at the porch screen.

Cora had never been much of a rocker, the creak and motion of the chair disturbing the quiet cherished by her father, but rocking proved to be a comfort those moments she had to herself. Her arms crossed on her front, since the chair was armless, she rocked with both feet on the floor, lifting her heels on the backswing. Orion had brought back from Columbus a small Axminster rug which she was at pains not to walk or rock on. The intricate pattern, in harmonious colors, provided the background for her thoughts. The glare and shimmer at the windows gave Cora headaches, but Emerson seemed to welcome the light in his face, a chair drawn up to the window while he sat shelling popcorn. Holding an ear of the corn in his injured hand, he would husk off the kernels with a cob. Whatever he did, shelling corn, husking peas, or sorting potatoes, some of it made its way to his mouth. In the evening, on the chair with springs, turned so the lamplight glowed behind him, he patiently read the operating instructions of his latest piece of machinery. After a period of concentration, he would say, "Who they expect to read print as fine as that?" and pass it on to Orion. It was left to Cora, after the brothers had haggled, to fill out the order blanks in the mail order catalogues and calculate the shipping charges. Neither brother had gone to school far enough for fractions, or what to do with the decimal point in multiplication. On the mailing envelope Cora's Spencerian hand was fine as the signatures seen on labels. Emerson had not known his wife was so accomplished when he married her.

As smart as she was, Emerson felt it necessary to read aloud to her from *Capper's Weekly,* his lips puckered to hold in his chew of tobacco. Politics interested Emerson, but he understood its complexities were beyond the grasp of women. On those points where he differed with Orion, or Senator Capper, Emerson would fold the paper and refuse to read further. He did not argue. In another man this might imply he was thinking, but in Emerson it meant the issue was settled. His gaze averted, he would use a kitchen match to clean the wax from his ears.

A bounty had been placed on wolves in the county, although neither Emerson nor Orion had seen one. Orion shot rabbits, but to tell the truth, it almost sickened Cora to clean and cook them. Stripped of its pelt, the taut body glistened. The small legs put her in mind of fingers. On her plate all she could think of was the pleading eyes. Somehow this did not trouble her about chickens, which she took the pains to behead herself, sometimes chasing the headless flapping bird around the chopping block. Orion plucked the bird for her, and the feathers were saved for a sleeping crib for Madge. They had pork from a neighbor, a pig raiser, who exchanged the cuts for eggs and butter,

Cora's way with the cream, after the separation, proving to be sweeter than customary. Orion would clean the rim of the crock with his finger, then lick it off.

Very briefly they had a problem with eggs, since Emerson firmly believed the yolk concealed a live but featherless chicken. His eggs had to be fried to the hardness of meat, and sliced with a knife, like cheese. Nothing would budge him. He would not touch an egg that he could penetrate with his fork's edge. Both Emerson and Orion liked their potatoes in a white sauce, their peas in a white sauce, and their biscuits served with pan gravy, the biscuits used to wipe the plate clean, like the tongue of a dog.

Cats appeared before stray dogs, however, prowling around the sheds, skulking across the yard, or furtively competing with the chickens for the food she threw out with the dishwater, hissing like snakes. Cora did not welcome cats, having heard of the way they stole the breath of babies asleep in their cradles, but Emerson, of all people, encouraged them to gather around him in the barn at milking time. A few would stand erect, exposing their undersides to be squirted with milk from the cow's teat, then draw back into the shadows to lick it off. He was not averse to dipping his hand into the frothing pail, then letting the cats lick it clean to the wrist. Along the trail from the barn to the house, both pails sweeping the weeds, the cats followed along so nimbly even Cora spied on them, their tails up stiff as a cane with a crook at the end. Time taken for such idle pleasure, although for just a moment, required that she apply herself harder to whatever she was doing, more pressure to the crank of the cream separator, the clothes wringer, or the handle of the broom. She was not one to criticize idleness in others and indulge in it herself.

Observation assured Cora that chickens were stupid, but how had she ever begun the day without them? They were *her* chickens: where they laid their eggs was her responsibility. Missing her from the house, or seeing her only dimly, a long striding phantom in the dusk of the evening, Orion understood she was looking for the eggs it seemed the purpose of the hens to hide. Brought into the house in the sling of her apron, they were stored in a syrup pail until Sunday, at which time, seated on the porch, she would remove the dung spots with a scrape of her thumbnail, then bury them in sawdust in the storm cave. Emerson would sell these eggs to a grocer in Battle Creek, and bring back to her, in silver, the proceeds. This was *her* money, which she stored in a bowl that might be used for sugar on special occasions. Joshingly Emerson asked her what she meant to do with it. Was that a mistake? When he came in from the fields a few weeks later, he found the porch screen latched and had to rap on it. His shoes were caked with field dirt. She asked him to take them off. Behind her he saw, gleaming as if wet, the linoleum that covered the floor of the kitchen, brightly colored as Christmas paper. Wasn't it to walk on? he asked. While it was new, she replied, they would walk on it with their shoes off. This proved to both clean it and give it a polish. Her pleasure in this possession was tempered by her knowledge that it bordered on display. Dr. Geltmayer was the first to walk on it in his shoes. With a cleverness that shamed her, Cora explained that the plank floor was drafty in the winter and the crawling child sometimes picked up splinters. It reassured her to learn that he had such refinements in his own house.

Often the chores were so demanding Cora simply lacked the time to churn the cream which was yellow as butter. Orion poured it like syrup on his pancakes; if it soured, he ate it spread on his biscuits. He washed both corn bread and her shortcake down his throat with gulps of buttermilk. From all of this, to her surprise, he suffered no ill effects. He took a boy's delight in the slip and suck of his boots in the deep manure of the cow manger, as thick and dark as chewed tobacco. In the open fields she often heard him singing at his work.

Nothing astonished her so much as watching Emerson with the child. He made faces with closed eyes, his thumbs in his ears, the fingers wagging as he brayed hee-haw like a donkey. He made a face with open eyes, the lips forming a round O, suddenly exploding in a loud *Ah-chooo!* that startled Beulah Madge silly. This gave her hiccups, which had to be treated by slapping her on the bottom until she burped, or letting her hang like a rabbit by the heels. He covered his face with his hands, peering at her through the slits between his fingers, her eyes so wide and staring Cora feared they might pop. Placed to straddle his knee, her tiny hands gripping his fingers, the child would bounce until she was dizzy. But if Cora said, "Here

34

now, I'll take her," how she would howl. It was comical how much she looked like him. Placed on her back in the crib, she would squirm in such a manner the hair was slow to grow at the crown of her head. It troubled Cora to see them both from the rear, their heads bald as targets. It also seemed to Cora that the child was slow to talk, but how would she know? During the church service other infants she saw either slept or howled, their faces red as cherries. When she hesitantly hinted at her concern, Emerson harumphed, pleased as if he had been tickled, reminding her that the problem with a female child was to shut them up once they started talking. Actually, it pleased her, on a trip to Battle Creek, to see the vanity he showed selecting a new straw hat, allowing the salesman to move around behind him so that he could see the rear view in a mirror. His hair had been cut, the scalp white as a bandage above his dark, weathered neck.

The summer chores were demanding, each day long and exhausting, but never long enough for her to catch up. Too tired to sleep, she would sometimes rise from bed and go below to sit in her rocker. In the moonlight the white trim on the barn's doors and windows stood free of the barn, and seemed to come toward her. It was eerie what she saw, or thought she saw, one night. Her husband, Emerson, moving like a sleepwalker, came down the stairs and passed unseeing before her, crossing the yard to the privy, where he sat with the door open, his legs white as paint. On his way back he paused to dip water from the pail and take several deep swallows, his Adam's apple pumping. It troubled Cora that he would seldom bother to skim off the flies. He had belched, then said, "What a woman needs is one thing, but what a farm needs is another." She had been too startled to reply. He spoke as if he saw her right there before him, at the door to the porch. She thought he meant to go on and she waited, hushed, while he tossed a dipper of water at the bugs cluttering the screen. Somewhere in the barn, or behind it, she heard the moaning caterwauling of the cats. Their piercing ear-splitting shrieks no longer dismayed her. How well she had come to understand it! Nothing known to her had proved to be both so bizarre and so repugnant as the act of procreation, but she understood that it was essential to its great burden of meaning. In the wild, cats shrieked. In the bedroom Cora had bitten through her hand to the bone. Dimly she gathered that Emerson, in speaking as he did, wanted her to know that she had failed him. What a farm needed was sons. She had borne a daughter, to be fed and clothed, then offered on the marriage market. Who would be there to run the farm as they grew old? Nothing in Emerson's nature assured her that he would not repeat the first experience, but the passage of time, the consoling rut of habit, had dulled the terror and anxiety she had once felt. He did not move toward her. He did not caress or strike her. He lay awake with his thoughts or he slept, or he snored, as if they had reached an understanding. Was she right in thinking he had spoken as he did to relieve her of the burden of his expectations? They were heavy within her. They weighed her down more than the child. Had he spoken to her as he did so that she would feel free to go back to bed, or so that she would share a burden too great for him to bear alone? She didn't know. It sometimes seemed to her she knew him less than if they had never met. Nevertheless, what had happened, or what had not happened, took on for her the importance of a religious ceremony: her feet seemed nailed to the floor, she could neither rock the chair nor rise from it. This awesome, aching silence would be broken by Emerson, scratching himself inside his underwear, then seeming to forget what time it was and taking the clock from the range to wind it, saying aloud, "Why, dang, I already done that," and proceeding upstairs.

The fall harvest was so abundant the temporary house was converted to a grain shed to store it. The doors were locked shut and the grain was shoveled through the stovepipe hole in the roof. Sacks of corn were stored in the loft of the barn and the upstairs bedrooms, attracting the mice, for which Cora set traps. More often than not these creatures proved to be so clever they set off the traps and ate the bait. Curious to observe the little thieves at their work, Cora lay awake, wide-eyed, her gaze fastened on the traps in the hallway. The mouse that set them off proved to be Orion. She heard him whispering and actually encouraging the mice. He would make scratching sounds on the floor to bring them out of their holes. Cora felt neither affection nor compassion for creatures that took from her what was rightfully hers. A mouse caught in the house, a rabbit in her garden, or a coon in her storm cave was an offense to her nature. Against the forces aligned against her she felt, like Emerson, there were no truces. If for a day or a night she faltered, they made measurable gains.

With his share of the crop Orion bought a saddle horse, a new Winchester rifle, and took off for the Ozarks. Even Cora was dismayed by such flaws in his nature: was he a hillbilly or a farmer? After three weeks he might have returned empty-handed if he had not had an accident while hunting. Stalking deer, Orion had crawled through a dense tangle of poison oak. Lacking experience with it he scratched, and the infection spread to all parts of his body, including his scalp. A local girl, Belle Rooney, immune to the poison, was wonderfully efficient in caring for him. Cora knew nothing of all this until they appeared, with his horse and a wagon piled with what they would need to begin housekeeping, although they had no house. A girl with coal-black hair and a hillbilly manner (the pitch of her voice deafened Cora), she cast her eyes about nervously as she talked; the front of her soiled blouse lacked buttons. Cora thought her wild and unkempt in appearance, her black hair disheveled as an unruly child's. She did not wear bloomers. Most of what little Cora had heard of hill people seemed confirmed.

Belle was not afraid of work, however, and couldn't seem to get enough of child caring and tending. She spent most of her day in Cora's dining room or kitchen, fondling and fussing with Beulah Madge. Orion explained her own mother was dead, and she had been the one to tend and raise six smaller children. She liked all babies, but she loved Beulah Madge. It was a great help to Cora to be free of child tending while there was so much to be done elsewhere. Emerson said, surprising her, that now she had an old one and a young one. With his own plowing to do, he was no help to Orion, who had to find a hired hand to help with the house building. One of them Scandahoovians, as Emerson called him, he came to and from Cora's table without a word. Of what extraction he was, if he had people somewhere, if he intended to settle or move on westward, neither Orion nor Cora heard him say, although he would nod his head in answer to questions. He took pains to empty and rinse his own wash pan, but a towel was soaked wet once he had wiped his hands, face, and huge ears. He started his hammering and sawing when there was light enough to see, and would work in the darkening twilight after supper. It was the same as having two men working different shifts. Of course, Orion, just as Emerson had feared, had to have himself a house with a basement, but as soon as the first floor was nailed down the hired hand made himself at home in it. It distressed Cora to see the way he carried nails in his mouth. A man who did that most of his life might find he had lost the power to speak his own language, whatever it was. What Orion paid him he put into his pocket and had no occasion or opportunity to spend. Just when Cora had grown accustomed to his presence at the table, he was gone, and she missed him, much as it had distressed her to see the sawdust at the roots of his hair when he bowed for grace.

With a place of her own, Belle Rooney still spent most of her day with Cora and Madge. She did what Cora told her, or she cunningly managed not to do it, as a clever child might. Brown sugar disappeared from the crock in the cupboard, and honey from the comb stored in the storm cave. Belle had cravings. "I just don't know what I'd do without sweeteners," she said, as if she ever did. She helped herself to change from the sugar bowl the way a child would take cookies from a jar in the pantry. With it she bought ribbons, pins, and cheap jewelry to make herself pretty. Cora was amazed. She could not understand this need for self-display. Nor when new buttons were attached to her blouse did Belle manage to keep them buttoned.

"Now look here," Cora would say, and button her up, but it left no impression. It vexed Cora, but did not make her angry. She might as well try to take a stitch in the weather. After all, there was no one to see her but Cora, Orion, and the grubbing Madge. Emerson seemed unaware that she was there. He had not been consulted in the matter of their marriage, and it was his way of ignoring that it had happened. A woman like Cora would have taken offense, but Belle was like a wild creature among those she liked, both friendly and indifferent to those who didn't like her. Not many, though, were indifferent; the men at the Sunday service followed her with their eyes.

Just as Emerson had warned them, a house with a basement only halfway beneath it looked strange. One had to go up a flight of four steps to the porch, which few women could do holding two pails of water. Holding nothing at all, a man could fall and break his leg. It put Emerson in mind of a Burlington caboose. All winter long, when the trees were bare, he would have no choice but to look at it. Every morning he would look at it, then say to Cora, "You think they plan to live in it?" The easygoing, patient side of Emerson was based on what he found to be customary, but a house that sat up on concrete blocks looked to him like something on a flatcar. He wished it was. He wished he could wake up and see it was gone.

A further affront was the notions that Orion had picked up somewhere about farming. He wanted no more chickens, since Cora had them, than he would need to keep a few fresh eggs on the table. Milk and cream he would get from Cora, so he wouldn't need cows. The only way you would know he was living in the country was the whine of the pigs when he fed them, and the smell they made when the wind died down. He kept so many pigs he had to buy swill and cart it from Battle Creek in a wagon. Behavior like that so disturbed Emerson he would talk at night. It was not to Cora, so she never knew if it was in his sleep, or awake and to himself. The discovery, which he made by chance, that Orion planned to enlarge the basement with the house already built above it was a thing so strange and imponderable to Emerson he could not find words to describe it. No, it stumped him. Standing before Cora, his gaze averted to the window that looked toward Orion, he would lift the front plate on the range and spit a gob on the fire that would crackle the corn shucks. That's how he felt, and that's all he could do to relieve his mind.

Before the windows were screened, or the porch built at the front, Belle Rooney's father came up from the Ozarks with three hound dogs in the seat of his buggy. The sad-eyed bitch of the three was about to litter. Mr. Rooney talked freely, with gestures of his hands, but Cora found it hard to understand him. Her feeling was that Belle's people were gypsies. He proved to know nothing to speak of about pigs or farming, but he had no objection to the people who did it. He lived on what he shot and the fish he caught, and he and Orion went hunting up the Elkhorn to shoot a few wolves and collect the bounty. They didn't see any wolves, but they brought back to Belle a baby raccoon which the hound bitch seemed willing to suckle. It disturbed Cora to think that such a sensible dog didn't know its own kind. After Mr. Rooney left, Emerson caught the coon at the back of the stable with one of Cora's chickens. Orion had the option to shoot it himself or take it back up the Elkhorn where he found it, which he claimed he did. It was during this summer that Cora worried what might rub off Belle onto Beulah Madge.

It turned out that Belle liked to make her own candles, and burned them more than she did the lamp. If Cora went over with a pan of biscuits, or a plate of fresh butter, she might find Belle running around the house barefoot, like a child. Her hair looked as if it might have birds nesting in it, and it worried Cora that she might have mites, and give them to Madge. It was also her custom, now that she had a few of her own, to let the chickens have the run of the house, as well as the hounds. A more irksome problem was the bitch, Lou, and her puppies, which she nursed in a box behind the range. If Cora spoke to Orion, he would put his head to one side and laugh. Something loose in his own nature seemed to be at ease with a girl like Belle. Nor was she any different when she proved to be pregnant and found it harder to hold and fondle Madge. As her breasts swelled, and her blouse gaped unbuttoned, it shamed Cora to admit what she was thinking. If left alone, she feared Belle would give her breast to Madge. Sensible as Cora was, she suffered the superstition that the wildness in Belle's nature might be there in her milk, corrupting the child. Belle had her own strange opinions and considered milk that had been separated no better than water, and fit only for pigs. If a pig was butchered, the pork had to be stored in its own fat. In these matters she stared at Cora with the eyes of a child at a side show, astonished by the freaks. The many things that Cora knew did not impress her, but what she didn't know defied accounting. Cora's patience was often so tried she pretended to sleep if Belle paid her a visit, but she was a godsend with the washing and had a man's strength cranking the wringer. Cora never seemed to tire of watching her string up the sheets, her face flushed and radiant with exertion, the clothespins in her mouth clamped so firmly she left her teeth marks on them. Everything she handled she had to smell before she put it down. Freshly washed and ironed clothes, a ladle of butter, berries and peas sorted for cooking, as well as both the laundered and the dirty diapers. She sniffed the child as well, running her finger in the folds of flesh before they were powdered, lidding her eyes as she held the finger to her nose. Yet it was Belle, surely, who taught Beulah Madge to talk. Cora picked her up, fed her, and put her down, but Belle would carry her about to look at the chickens, or into the barn while Emerson was milking, all the time babbling her shrill hillbilly talk. Cora hoped that such speech would come slow to Madge, but even the chickens might learn it if they heard enough of it. She marveled at a creature who was at once so ignorant and so alive. In midmorning, her chores finished, she would come running through the trees between the two houses more like a frightened calf than a young woman. Cora could hear her coming. The next moment there she would be, standing at the screen like an anxious puppy. Her manner suggested that Cora had called her, her cheeks red as a fever. She wore a shift made of flour sacks, and would lift her skirts to wipe her hands clean on the underside.

"Where's she at?" she would ask, and look around as if Cora had hidden *her* baby. What Belle liked about caring for a child was seeing how everything worked; where and what went in, and if and what came out, was to her of great importance. She had nobody but Orion to tell her she shouldn't take such an interest in another woman's child. Why didn't Cora tell her? She simply didn't feel the interest that Belle felt. She felt duties toward the child, and concern for her, but was not so eager as Belle to hug, fondle, and pet her. In her childish way Belle was cruel to Cora, fingering her blouse buttons even while she was prattling, but that was through ignorance, not intent. Yet seeing them together, Belle curling her finger to offer the child the nub of her knuckle to suckle, Cora knew that in this matter Belle was not to be trusted. She knew that and admired it, feeling shame for this lack in herself.

For all her prattling, Belle told Cora little about herself. Her darting blackberry eyes (Orion's description) were made to look all around her but not within her. Like a child, watching Cora at her ironing, she would pick the buggers out of her nose. Her glances were not so cruel as indifferently curious, passing over the flatness of Cora's bust, her jaw slack as she strained to visualize how she must look in her nightshirt, a picture that Cora took pains not to gratify. She would have liked someone like Mrs. Geltmayer to give her an opinion of Belle. A good enough girl, but wild. Something like that. Orion would be the one to know her best, but it was unthinkable that Cora might ask him. Compared with Emerson, he still seemed youthful. Did his strange young wife perhaps confess to him, at night, that she would like to nurse Cora's child before the bottle had rotted its teeth or impoverished its nature? In her soul Cora knew that Belle would do whatever came naturally.

In the Ozarks Belle had been accustomed to Sunday being more social. She saw all of her relations. Sunday without them was simply not Sunday. In the side yard of the church she played with the children, scuffing the toes of her good Sunday shoes. Orion could not restrain her. He could only wait until she tired. "She's like a rabbit," he would say, as they watched her, but it was one of many words he applied to Belle. Riding home in the buggy, she would fall to sucking on a strand of her hair. Her habit of thrusting out her lower lip and blowing a cooling draft of air up her face provoked Cora. Cora had seen to it that the cats stayed in the barns, where they paid for their keep and were useful, only to find that Belle came to her for milk she carried back to her house and fed stray kittens. They were everywhere. Did she understand that kittens grew up to be cats? It seemed to Cora she was much too young to be a mother, although not too young, obviously, to become one, her tummy protruding at her front like a baby's. Nobody at all, unless it was Belle, proved to be prepared for it when it came, such a little thing it gave her no trouble. Being another girl, it annoyed Emerson. She was named Sharon Rose, after Belle's mother. She proved to be a black-haired, fair-skinned child with a birthmark where nobody would be likely to see it. The way the child nursed with her eyes wide open disturbed Cora. By her own calculation the child came five weeks early, which made her an easier baby to handle, nor did it cross Cora's mind that there might be a flaw in her calculations. Sharon Rose was Belle's baby. Orion seemed to have little to do with it.

Only in the first summer of their acquaintance did Madge, in Cora's opinion, enjoy an advantage over Sharon Rose. She had her to watch, and on occasion to whack with the wooden spoon she loved to chew on. Soon enough Sharon Rose would take the initiative.

A squirming, obstinate child, she wanted down if she was lifted, she wanted lifting if she was down, on her back if she was on her stomach, on her stomach if she was on her back, resistant to stroking, quick to fret, pull on beads, hairpins, ear lobes, and hairnets, waking at night to shriek in such a manner even Emerson took note of it. In his opinion it was only early babies that howled like that. It made Cora grateful for Madge, who would be silent until she was banged by Sharon Rose. If Cora placed a netting over the crib she would drop off to sleep, like a bird in a cage. Out the window, in the space of one summer, went all the talk she had heard about bottle babies, little Sharon Rose, even in Orion's opinion, nursing as if she meant to eat Belle alive. If she was raised from the floor, she would paw at Belle until she was nursed. It shamed Cora to hear Emerson say, "Put that one in the barn and she'd find the milk tit."

Because the plump Madge hardly seemed to care, and would as soon look at Sharon as not look at her, it seemed sensible, even to Cora, to treat the two girls as one. Belle would either come over and pick up Madge, or she would bring Sharon Rose along with her, Madge seated like a bucket on her fat bottom while Sharon Rose crawled, squirmed, and fretted around her. Madge's hand-me-downs were large, but so much the better for Sharon Rose to grow into. In Belle's house, which still lacked curtains, the little girls were put on the rugless floor and given blocks to play with. Floor splinters turned up in both knees and diapers. Belle said she found the shrieks and howls reassuring, a sign of life. For several weeks the girls shared the same bottle, Belle's nipple being too sore and chapped for nursing. Cora would not have liked that if she had heard it, but she didn't hear. The babies had their runny, snotty colds together, and their runny, smelly diapers together, but an early blizzard, followed by a heavy snow, kept the girls apart during most of January. The drift of snow between the two farms was more than five feet deep. In March Sharon Rose had a rash about her nose and mouth, and Belle was subject to morning sickness and a nagging cough. She was expecting again, but it seemed reasonable to assume that this one would be a nine months' baby. It was a bad time for Cora, the winter breaking, the whole yard like a pond with the ice melting, and it might be that her feelings for Sharon Rose were not as friendly as back in November. The rash made her fretful and demanding. Did she sense Cora's reluctance to pick her up? She fell silent, rather than quiet. Missing her howling, her fretting, Cora would have to stop her work and go find her. Often she would be under the dining room table, concealed by the cloth that hung to the casters, a look of cunning and satisfaction behind her long, tangled lashes. In the eyes of Madge one saw only the window reflections. It absorbed her to watch and ponder Sharon Rose as the hound bitch Lou watched and pondered Orion oiling and cleaning his guns.

Although a nine months' child, Eula Stacy Atkins weighed even less at her birth than Sharon Rose. Nor was the third female child to be fathered by an Atkins a cause for rejoicing to Emerson. Was it a jinx? he asked Dr. Geltmayer. Belle was soon up and about, but the same milk that was so good for Sharon Rose gave Eula the worst kind of colic. A wet nurse in Battle Creek took the child during April, but when Belle got her back she didn't feel right about her. She was able to nurse her, part time, but Eula would only suckle in the bed at night, as if she didn't want to see whom she was nursing. Nor did she take well to napping with her sister, or find it absorbing to watch Madge. This new baby took all of Belle's attention, much of her sleep, yet she never really felt as she should about it. She was surely wrong in thinking, and admitted to thinking, that Eula thought the wet nurse, Mrs. Raike, was her mother, and she, Belle, was just her wet nurse. But she was right in thinking, in Dr. Geltmayer's opinion, that Mrs. Raike wanted the child for herself. That was only natural. Her own child had died at birth, and she had milk in her breasts that pained her. Belle confided to Cora that such women were able to put a hex on the nursing baby, so that it was only the milk of the wet nurse they liked. Cora had met Mrs. Raike, a huge, sad woman who tilted the buggy getting up and down from it, speaking only German to the hired hand who brought her to church. Mr. Raike was a freethinker and an agnostic.

In late May, after a night of wailing brought on by an attack of colic, Eula just died as Belle sat and rocked her. It was so like she had dropped off to sleep it didn't upset Belle as much as it should have. Sleep and death were so alike at times it was hard to tell one from the other, and in the case of Eula it might have been Belle's choice. Belle had blurted that out herself, and then gone right on as if she hadn't said it. Orion would sit and not hear much that she said unless he was assured what it might be, averting his gaze, like Emerson, to what he might see out the window. Without confiding in Cora, without consulting Emerson, without so much as discussing it with each other, they buried little Eula at the far back of their pasture under a tree that shaded some of the neighbor's cows. The grave was not marked. Cora knew only what she was told. Emerson heard this from her, as he did everything, working a straw between his teeth, his blinking gaze averted, saying aloud to himself, rather than to Cora, that Orion no longer had the wits he was born with because of that girl. He did not say, but Cora knew he was thinking that Belle had worked a spell on Orion. She and her crazy hillbilly family were given to ignorant habits and superstitions. To bury a child without a service, like a dog or a cat, was a heathen act. It was against God's law and common sense to bury a child in a grave without a marker. Before the summer was over they would never be able to find it. Was that their intent? Since Orion had married, and built his wacky house, and let other people do his farming for him, Emerson failed to understand his brother and he wasn't so sure he any longer felt obliged to.

Cora was troubled at night by the thought of the child lying in the cold earth. Had they put it in a box? Or had they merely wrapped it in the flour and sugar sacks used for dishcloths? She wanted to know, but she dreaded to hear what Belle might say. She was shocked too deeply to speak about it, yet she understood in her soul what had happened. Belle had not liked the child. She wanted to forget that it had ever existed. The way some animals destroyed the weak members of the litter, Belle did not want this child to make demands on her. Her nature was sure. It told her without confusion how she should act. What could be done for those, and Cora feared there were many, who did not distinguish between right and wrong? What could be done for those who were able to distinguish but chose to do wrong? If Belle had cast a spell over Orion its shadow could be seen hovering over Cora, who saw plainly as a crack in a plate the strengths and weaknesses of her own nature. She was God-fearing. But there were things in this world that scared her even worse.

It was hardly surprising that Belle grew more possessive of both Sharon Rose and Madge. She would put the two girls in a wicker wash basket and tow them to her house on a wooden runner sled. Madge was such a plump, fat child she caused Belle to grunt when she was lifted from the floor. Sharon Rose was almost frail, but her pretty little mouth was seldom shut. She was also selfish, in the way of most children, and took from Madge whatever she had been given, but since Madge didn't seem to mind, she soon gave it back. She seemed to be less acquisitive than domineering, yet when she dominated she soon lost interest. If not assured that children grew into grownups, Cora would have been appalled by what she saw. If deprived of Madge, Sharon Rose would howl as if in pain. There were things Cora saw that she refused to admit, turning away to fuss with something, look for eggs, or stand in the dark of the stairwell for a moment, her apron pressed to her face. Both children proved to eat paint, where it flecked, and the soft muck where the dishwater was emptied. Without something in her mouth, Sharon Rose babbled in a singsong voice, almost like a bird warbling, but it also signified the filling of her diaper with number two. She was Belle's child, Cora reasoned with herself, and let her squirm in it.

With or without the little girls, Cora's chores were never done. She tooks eggs to Battle Creek to be hatched in the incubator, and brought back the chicks to swell her flock of Plymouth Rocks. Emerson had built her some sheds, with a fenced-in run for the chickens, hoping to keep the cackling hens away from the house, but what he proved to have done was to have drawn a line between his farm and Cora's yard. The yard included her chickens, the pump on its platform, the storm cave along the path that led to the pump, and as much as half an acre of grass and weeds. One day Emerson came in from the field to find the weeds scythed between the house and her sheds.

"You folks run out of steam?" he asked her. The way Emerson took a dig at Cora was to include her in with Belle and Orion. He had come to the house with two pails of water, which he lowered to the ground, then turned to look behind him. One could see very plainly where the cut grass ended and the weeds began.

"I've grass in mind for the yard," Cora said, "not weeds."

"I take it you know the difference," Emerson replied. He didn't turn to see if she did: he waited to hear.

"It's been scythed," Cora said, "but what I plan to do is mow it."

Enough time passed to allow the water to settle in both pails. "I guess it's your yard," he said, stooping for the pails, and she held the screen open until he had entered, "but don't you ask me what you plan to do for horsepower," and she never did. It was her yard, it would be her grass, and she would manage to care for what was hers.

Already the yard had some shade from the trees near the house. As the hedge grew taller she would be able to walk from the house to the pump out of the sun glare. Cora seldom left the house without a bonnet. The worst possible complexion for this country was the one she had brought with her. Just a ride in the buggy and the skin of her nose dried and peeled. In her outdoor chores she wore cotton work gloves; if it rained she wore Emerson's two-buckle galoshes. At no time did it cross her mind how she might look. Against the cool morning air she would slip on the coat or sweater not worn that day by Emerson. The tobacco odor that saturated his clothes was not disagreeable to her in the open. It neutralized the acrid smell of the henhouse. Without clearly grasping why, Cora had felt dispersed, her workday too short to deal with the end-less chores of the farm, but once she had determined her own domain she could see what each day had accomplished.

On the backside of the cobhouse, where it was

sunny and windless, she cleared the ground for a seedbed and a garden. Emerson was not lazy, but anything he hadn't done the day before, or had to be told to do, he had to ponder. Orion plowed it into furrows for her while Emerson was making up his mind. Right away he disagreed with what Orion had done, but it was too late. He was good with the cows, as Orion wasn't—they would moo and balk whenever he came near them—but if Emerson stuck his head into the henhouse the hens would stop laying. The cackling might go on far into the night. It worked better if everybody had their place, Belle helping with the washing and the children, Cora in the house and yard, Emerson in the barn and the fields. One thing he did better than anybody else was sit in the yard, on Sunday, with the babies, or lie out on his back and let them crawl and paw over him. Belle startled Cora by saying, "He wouldn't do that for long if they was boys, not girls." This saying tantalized Cora, but it provoked her more than it pleased her. Why would the lumbering Emerson, like a big friendly dog, rather be crawled on by two little girls than by boys? It was Belle's way to blurt out remarks Cora was slow to forget.

Emerson didn't spoil the girls, the way Belle did, or make a fuss over them in the manner of Orion, who scared their mothers half to death the way he'd take Sharon Rose and swing her by the heels. She shrieked when he did it, making a sound like a calliope. As the summer ran down, Cora found the time to sit, after washing the dishes, on the cool of the porch. In the evening hush, the chickens quiet, she could hear

Emerson muttering to his cows and the squirt and froth of milk in the pail. Madge slept in a clothes basket, free of the tireless Sharon Rose, and Cora was free of Belle's ceaseless prattle. More and more, it seemed to Cora, Belle's prattle was less an expression of her high animal spirits than a need to break the silence around her. Orion took his hounds and went off hunting whenever he could.

Cora had tried, and failed, to put a stop to the cats' following Emerson and his milk pails to the house. She had her chickens, he said to her, he had his cats. While they waited at the screen, he would crank the separator, then put the pail into the yard for them to lick clean. He would wash himself, using her yellow soap, lathering his face and neck but staying clear of his ears, wetting her floor as he splashed himself with water, blowing and wheezing like he was drowning. He would empty what water was left through the screen, then stand there drying his face and hands, watching the label of the Pillsbury flour appear on the wet cloth. At that point, if he thought it might rain he would say so, otherwise he was quiet.

Orion made the little girls dolls out of corncobs, with tassels of long taffy-colored hair. Belle sewed them up bean bags, with rag doll faces, that came with the sacks of flour and sugar. Cora had surely not lacked dolls as a child, but she frowned on the attention the little girls gave them. Madge seemed more content with her dolls than Sharon Rose. Was that because they were silent, and would listen to *her?* Both little girls spent hours hiding in the cobhouse just to annoy Cora. Belle seemed like a child herself, the way she would cry out and get excited. The word "Shar'n!" was like a bird's cry in her shrill, high-pitched voice. Of course, the child never answered. She was usually to be found behind the sacks of popcorn that were waiting for Emerson to shell them. Belle was fearful for Sharon whenever she was missing, but took little comfort in her presence now that she was expecting. "What would she do with another girl?" Emerson asked. What might she blurt out to a question like that?

Belle had spells of moodiness, and Orion might wake up and find her missing, and have to search for her. Walking about at night relieved her. Seated with Cora, a basket of mending between them, she would fall asleep. Neither Sharon Rose nor Madge held her attention, and she seemed indifferent to Orion. It was Cora who would find him, and put a plate at the table for him. Two days before Christmas Orion was off somewhere, hunting, when Belle began her labor. Before Emerson could fetch anybody, she gave birth to a child with Orion's blond hair, a birthmark on the left forearm. It seemed so frail and lifeless Cora feared it might be dead. Dr. Geltmayer arrived, but nothing he could do would stop Belle's internal bleeding. She died peaceful, looking like a young girl with tangled hair and a deathly pallor. She shouldn't have had another baby so soon, Dr. Geltmayer said. If Belle could have spoken up for herself, what would she have said to that? Cora wondered. A Bohemian girl, who still talked her own language, came from her people near

Blair to help with the new baby. She was a strong girl, and a good worker, but her strange speech confused the little girls. If Orion had had his own way, would he have buried his wife on the farm? Emerson thought so, and said so, and the brothers were so close to blows Cora threw dippers of water on them. Orion left the farm and was not seen again until the day before Washington's birthday, coming back from the Ozarks with a new saddle horse and three more hound dogs.

Cora had fretful, squalling children to care for in the face of Emerson's fury. She could hear him cursing to himself as he milked the cows. What had begun as a pig farm was now Orion's dog farm, but the folly of it relieved Emerson's anger. That, and the fact that he knew Orion was crazy. He had been crazy to marry a hill girl in the first place, and what had rubbed off on him had only made him worse. He was good for nothing but shooting off his guns and living with his dogs.

The new girl, Anna Pilic, would have made a good wife, but Orion seldom set his eyes on her. He left his house if she came over to clean it, and cooked his own meals. For her part, Anna Pilic could not lose her fear of his dogs. She did not ask, but Cora sensed that she wondered what sort of woman it was who had lived with them in her house. What sort of woman Belle was, from where she had come (even her age was unknown to Orion), and why she had departed in the manner she did, leaving the child nameless and unknown to her, occupied much of Cora's thought. She could not accustom herself to Belle's being dead. Cora missed her, in the hot, steaming kitchen, or running like an animal between the houses, her hair wild, her blouse forever unbuttoned, so vibrantly alive to think of her as dead was unthinkable. At night Cora listened for the snap of the twigs and the drag of her dress as she approached the porch. If Cora lifted Sharon Rose, she would hear Belle cry, "I'll take her! I'll take her!" since it was known she resisted Cora. But with Belle gone it seemed to Cora that Sharon Rose made less fuss.

Nothing would persuade Cora to terrify the little girls with the caged wild animals at a circus, but against her better judgment she went with Orion and Anna Pilic—Emerson scoffed at the thought of it—to the Chautauqua in Nehigh. In the dark of the tent, hung with smoking lanterns, she saw scenes from *Uncle Tom's Cabin,* Little Eva, to Cora's great relief, escaping from Simon Legree across the blocks of ice. (She did it on a rope that swung her, like an angel, from one bank of the river to the other.) Anna Pilic was so excited she sometimes put both hands to her eyes. Sharon Rose and Madge observed it all in silence, Sharon's eyes as bright as candles. Neither slept a wink on the long ride home, the night filled with the creak of the buggy, the clop-clop of the horse.

For days Cora was distracted with the thought of a world so near, yet so far. The only black woman she had ever set eyes on had been in Omaha, near where they crossed the river. Cora had little desire to see more than she had already seen, or feel more than she had already felt. The crowding of so many people into one great tent had been more disquieting than pleasurable, with the squealing of the boys and girls under the seats like mice in a shaken basket of cobs.

Anna Pilic was good with the little girls, but her strange speech troubled Cora. When she spoke to them, what was she saying? Sharon Rose often prattled it back. When Anna sang to them, Cora listened, pondering what she heard. Anna's love of music touched her, and brought to Cora's mind pleasures she had forgotten. Singing need not be confined to the church, but might be played and enjoyed in the home. The wife of her uncle, in Ohio, owned and played a foot-pedaled pump organ. In the catalogues Cora browsed in, when she had a moment, both pianos and organs were offered for sale that would play by themselves or could be played on the keys in the ordinary manner. She spent weeks wondering just where in the house it should sit. The living room offered a corner, free of windows, where it might sit at an angle facing the listeners. Both Orion and Emerson might be encouraged to spend more time there. Nor did she consult Emerson in this matter, since she would make the purchase with her own egg and butter income. That would help explain why, when it arrived, so little thought had been given as to how to get it into the house. The unused door at the front had to be taken off its hinges, and a ramp built to slide the piano from the wagon. Orion supervised the move, in Emerson's absence, and was the first to sit on the stool that came with it, and puzzle over the directions. He was mechanically minded, if not musical. Ten player rolls had come with it, in their boxes with the labels, and before

Emerson had come in from the field and paused at the barn to ponder what he was hearing, Anna Pilic had mastered the art of sitting on the stool seat while pedaling, and reversing the music to the point where it started. The volume proved to be deafening. Cora had left the house to let the breeze cool her flushed face. In the outdoors it was less alarming, and she could give attention to what she was hearing. Where had she heard it before? Her mouth went dry and her eyes filmed over, as they did when listening to hymns. She did not fully grasp what she had done until she saw Emerson transfixed at the barn door, assuring her that for a family limited to girls she had chosen right.

As he did when bewildered, Emerson stood gazing at the swallow-streaked sky. He liked birds. In the field he often paused to attend their song. He listened till he felt sure he knew what it was and that he had nothing to fear from it. After Belle little would surprise him, even if it was a man who did it. Before proceeding toward the house he stopped to wet his face at the pump.

The nearest school being a mile and a half due east, on a road that often disappeared during the winter, the Atkins girls did not attend school until they were big enough to walk it. Almost seven, Madge delayed for a semester while she waited for Sharon Rose to grow bigger. Madge was not tall, but she was chubby, and seemed to be impervious to heat and cold. She might forget to put the mittens, on cords to her sleeves, back on her hands if they happened to slip off. With the first thaws of spring, she would take off her shoes and wear them around her neck on the tied laces. She seemed to be made of a different material than Sharon Rose. If it was hot, Sharon Rose suffered from prickly heat, and her face would be flushed with streaks of color. If it was cold, her lips turned blue as a cake of ice. Anyone who saw her took pity on her and led her forward to a place near the fire, where, in no time at all, she suffered from the heat and would have to withdraw.

Madge's eyes were thought to be like buttons, or raisins stuck into the dough of a raw sugar cookie. For the whites of her eyes to be seen, she had to hold her breath until they nearly popped. In contrast, the orbs of Sharon Rose were so large it stretched the lids thin to conceal them. Was this one of the reasons she seldom blinked? She also had the disconcerting habit of sleeping with her eyelids half open, revealing only the whites. In the winter, her little face a snow mask, she was more like a trapped wild creature than a person, the blue of her eyes so intense they looked black. Seated at the table, or in one of the small front seats of Miss Mittlehofer's schoolroom, Sharon Rose returned each gaze without blinking. Of course, some children are like that, but not in the manner of Sharon Rose. Miss Mittlehofer sometimes feared she might stop blinking altogether. What it did was give her an air of composure that others found disturbing. Nervous little boys would turn from her gaze to run hooting around her like puppies. Seated at her desk, her little hands clasped in a manner that was not at all childlike, her eyes would follow Miss Mittlehofer with spellbound attention. One might observe the same thing in retarded children, or those proved to be hard of hearing. Sharon Rose, however, carried tunes in her head she heard only once. In a small, shrill voice, she would recite the multiplication tables as if they were jingles. Nor was it the usual defects that led Sharon Rose to impress her peers as something special. Her nose bled without being thumped, and she ate snow like it was sugar. Madge was so average no one would have seen her if she hadn't been there, looking after Sharon Rose. A puppy and a kitten would hardly have been stranger together than this plump child and her companion. People had to be told they were cousins, not sisters, but when one or the other was mentioned, they were known as the Atkins girls. Fayrene Dee, poor thing—named by Orion after one of Belle's sisters—might as well have been in another family. Cora was too busy to stand in one place long enough for the child to get a grip on her. Madge and Sharon Rose were enough for Emerson, who considered Fayrene one girl too many. Orion lived with his dogs, and Cora could see in his manner that he blamed the child for Belle's death.

Madge and Sharon Rose were so used to each other they resented sharing anything with Fayrene, especially Sharon Rose. The cruelness of children astonished Cora, since it seemed so at odds with their gentle natures. Sharon Rose would go out of her way to give Fayrene pain. It perplexed Cora to sense that the punishment she gave Fayrene pleased her. Was it the wild blood of her hillbilly mother? It meant nothing to her that Fayrene was her sister. Being so much alone, Fayrene was slow to talk. She attached herself to Emerson, who didn't want her, but out of habit he became accustomed to her, even though she reminded him of Orion. The child would toddle after him in the yard, or let him spoon-feed her at the table. If Emerson scooped her up, Sharon Rose would squeal and ask to be put down. She didn't like to be tickled, or have her face scratched by Emerson's beard. Tickling her, he once said, "You a cat or a kitten?"

"I'm a cat!" she cried, and clawed her little hands at him. Emerson made light of it, pinching her bottom, but it was the last time he scooped her up. It was no loss to Sharon Rose, but a real gain for Fayrene.

Whenever he had the chance, Emerson liked to say that when he came in from the field he wondered whose farm it was. People who knew Cora could believe that. There were three girls in the family, no sons, and a gasoline motor now pumped the water that was piped across the yard to her garden. The next thing he knew, it would sprinkle her grass. What she had in mind, and had explained to Orion, was water enough to flush a toilet inside the house. What difference would there be between the farm and the city if people kept it up?

At the state fair in Lincoln she had seen a gas-run contraption that would light up a house, and that would be next. For himself, Emerson didn't want it. The bulbs burned out, they were too bright to read by, and you couldn't turn them up and down like a lamp, only on and off. It pleased him to say that to people and listen to the comments that followed, no other woman, known to them personally, being more highly respected than Cora. She churned the best country butter, she raised the best sweet corn, and her new white Leghorn eggs ran larger and cleaner than those from the dairy people in Columbus. Of all she made, she never spent a nickel on herself.

Player rolls of the better class of music were piled five tiers high on the top of the piano, and the noise that once seemed deafening was music to which she had grown accustomed. The stout-legged Madge could pump it by sitting far forward and gripping under the keyboard to give her leverage, but Sharon Ro e could sit erect on the stool and tinkle out pieces using all ten of her fingers. It was not to be believed, but she did it, with the help of Ernst Kreidel, a piano tuner. He would sit or stoop beside her, humming the tunes, reading the music, until Sharon Rose caught on to it. She was a *Wunderkind,* he said, meaning no harm. Not to intrude upon them, two fingers at her lips, the left hand supporting the right arm at the elbow, Cora would stand at the door to the kitchen in a transport of wonder. That the piano played by itself she accepted. These were intricacies beyond her grasping. But that Sharon Rose sat there, her thin legs dangling, much too short to reach the pedals, and with her tiny hands made this music, reassured Cora that divine power might reveal itself in what was merely human. The plump Madge, careful to make no disturbance, stood at the door with its oval pane of glass, one of her chubby fingers tracing the etched floral pattern. The only special interest Madge seemed to have was

Sharon Rose. After the lesson the children would sit in the cobhouse and play with their dolls.

Cora's efficient way of doing things for herself was not, perhaps, the best way to bring up female children. Told to fetch cobs, Madge and Sharon Rose might be gone for half an hour. Madge was willing, of course, but she was easily distracted, and watching Sharon Rose was her special talent. The girls were good at pulling taffy, making popcorn, coloring Easter eggs, and scraping the inside of the fudge pan. Cora could not rest herself while listening to the sounds of others at work. Madge would surely have learned to sew and mend faster, but Sharon Rose's little fingers, so nimble on the keyboard, burned themselves, cut themselves, and dropped things without handles like plates and eggs. Knowing it would happen, Cora was soon there to shoo them out of the kitchen and clean up the mess. Sometimes the little girls could be heard giggling beneath the cloth that covered the dining room table, poor little Fayrene wondering what it was all about. Actually, she was more at her ease with the grownups, who lifted her to their laps or sat her on the backs of horses, than she was with the puzzling world of her sister. Why did she giggle? Fayrene was too young to know, too shy to ask.

These were good years for Cora. Many things confirmed her feeling that the rightness of their lives was His rightness. Chickens, people, and eggs had their appointed places, chores their appointed time, changes their appointed seasons, the night its appointed sleep. Emerson exhibited hogs and apples at the fair in Lincoln, from where he returned with his face nicked by a barber. He liked to lie out horizontal in the chair, with a hot towel on his face, and be raised or lowered. It seemed to Cora he belched less at the table now, and deferred to her in moments of decision. At the stove, where he scratched his matches, or at the screen, where he dried his hands, he might ask her opinion on the Leghorns as layers. It would be his opinion when she heard it next.

When Cora came to the screen, fanning the dead air with her apron, and gazed across the green lawn with its pattern of posts and wickets, the striped balls gleaming like eggs painted for Easter, the sad keening of the mourning doves filled her with a sorrowful pleasure, more satisfying to her nature than a blithe, careless happiness. In the chill of the morning, or the cool of the evening, the air heavy with the drone of insects, Cora's contentment might be so great it aroused her guilt. What had she done to be favored with such peace of mind?

At the school on Friday afternoons, Sharon Rose played music with Leah Sobotka, who could read and write in English but hardly speak it. Leah wore her yellow hair in braids that often got in the way as she played the cello. Madge would stand at the piano and turn the pages of the music for Sharon. It vexed Emerson to hear how little interest Madge showed in boys. She was now a plump, strapping girl, and when she put up her hair she looked like a young woman. Sharon Rose he put clean out of his mind when she visited a friend, in Columbus, and came back with her hair cut like a man's, short at the back.

Fayrene had the room off the kitchen to herself, hot in the summer but cozy over the winter. When she heard the creak of the boards in the ceiling, she opened up the stove drafts, put kerosene on the cobs and water in the kettle, and went back to bed. Time had proved that it was best to let Cora light the fire and start the day by herself. Both of the older girls stayed out of the kitchen till the food was cooked.

Cora was so long accustomed to doing things by herself she found it irksome if someone tried to help her. She carried her elbows high, even with her hands empty, and often caught the girls where they claimed to be tender. The meal might be delayed while they waited for Emerson to make his way back from the outbilly, wash and dry his hands, then drink the pitcher of buttermilk to relieve his stomach. In his own opinion he suffered from the weight of undigested cuds of chewing tobacco. They weighed on him at night, but after drinking the buttermilk, and several rumbling belches, they were gone. Whether Sharon Rose said that Emerson should eat with his pigs, or said something that merely implied it, it was Cora's house and a compromise was reached that he would drink his buttermilk away from the table. Emerson didn't let it rile him. A girl with Belle as a mother and Orion for a father could be expected to act mighty peculiar. Cora served hot biscuits, on the flat side, oatmeal cooked to the texture of taffy, cream thick as syrup, eggs fried hard in bacon grease, bread, butter, honey, and coffee. Except for grace, said by one of the girls, there was no talk. In the winter a lamp burned at the center of the table, the wick curled in a pool of oil, the flame reflected in the orbs of Sharon Rose like those of a cat. Emerson couldn't tell you whether she blinked or not, since he wasn't going to pay her that kind of attention. If she thought people might stare at her she wouldn't blink at all.

It was Orion's custom, in the midmorning, to stop and warm himself in Cora's kitchen. He might eat what the girls had left over, or she might stir up a batter and make him some flapjacks. It troubled her to think what sort of life he led in his own house. When she went over to change his sheets she would find dog hair on everything she touched. The Bohemian girl, Anna, who had surely been willing, married a widower in Olney with five small children, three of them girls. Cora could not sort out in her mind if this was man's or God's injustice. Piled along the wall beside Orion's bed were magazines with stories about the Wild West, full of cowboys and Indians, as well as tales of adventure in faraway places. Cora had stooped to glance at the illustrations. What life had been like before she came to the plains she feared to know about.

Orion loved to shoot his guns—Cora could hear the crack of his rifle, like a winter branch snapping—but he had stopped bringing her what he had killed. She saw the pelts stretched on racks in the basement. To bring her a moose rug—it was his way of joshing—he took off to hunt in Canada, with Ned Kibbee, a Norfork carpenter. Three weeks later Ned Kibbee returned alone. Where was Orion? He had gone to war.

But who had he found to go to war with? There was a war in Europe, Ned Kibbee explained, and Orion had signed up to help the Canadians, who were taking the side of the English. He had acted the way he did fearing it might be over before he got into it. What he liked about a war was the free ammunition, and a place to shoot. Nor would it be a long one, in Ned Kibbee's opinion, with young men like Orion so willing and eager to fight it. During the time he was away Ned Kibbee would be free to live in his house and look after his dogs.

The war did not end, as Ned Kibbee had predicted. From what she heard and read in *Capper's Weekly*, Cora learned that Americans would soon bring it to a quick conclusion. They had one letter from Orion, mailed from England, in which he asked for chocolate and tobacco. He had never used tobacco. Perhaps he had asked for it for a friend. It was all so far away Cora did not know what to think. Ned Kibbee enlisted, rather than be drafted, and went to Fort Riley, Kansas, for his training. When he stopped writing, Madge thought he had gone to war, but instead he had come down with the influenza. Madge went down to help nurse him. Half the people in the fort were sick, and many died. The first armistice declared was false, but a real one was determined and the war was over before Ned Kibbee got to fight in it.

Without a word of any kind, Orion was seen in the streets of Battle Creek, where Dr. Geltmayer recognized him and brought him to the farm. Cora thought the stranger at the door was a salesman. He wore rumpled city clothes, and his voice and manner had changed. Emerson wasn't sure it was his own brother until they had sat and talked a bit together. He had been gassed in the war. Most of his time had been spent in hospitals. His eyes moved from side to side as he talked. He knew Sharon Rose and Madge, and the names of his dogs, but he seemed to have forgotten about Fayrene. Speaking to the girls, he said, "Yes, ma'am," or "No, ma'am," as if they were young ladies. He was at ease with Cora, picking up where they had been when he left.

At the table he might have long spells of wheezing, his red face filmed with perspiration, his eyes popped. He never mentioned the war, but he spoke of friends and places in England. In the hospital he had learned to play cards and do tricks with coins. In spite of the tremor of his hands he could stand a dime on its edge on a table. Fayrene never tired of the way he could tilt a quarter back and forth on the back of his knuckles. If Ned Kibbee and Madge went to a movie in town, he went along for the ride. Cora was told, but she did not believe, that he had a manicure while he was being shaved. Later he would stand in the hotel lobby playing dice for cigars.

Because he was disabled in the service of his country he received a pension he could live on. He had always been so gentle with women he behaved as if he was courting. He brought Cora bars of clear glycerin soap she put away for a special occasion, if one should occur. He gave to the girls boxes of Whitman's chocolates, with the flavors printed in the box lids. This discouraged Sharon Rose from biting into something, then putting it back. Cora kept to herself the fact that Orion relieved himself from the porch, rather than troubling to walk to the privy. It worried Cora that the girls might see him, since he often seemed unaware of their presence. Madge was now a young lady, with a beau, but when Sharon Rose used the outbilly, at night, she liked Madge to go along with her and wait in the dark. Cora herself would have preferred to be frightened rather than suffer the humiliation of an escort. Sharon Rose was at once fearless and as timid as a child.

The day Sharon Rose came back from Lincoln, where she had gone to enroll in the university, she was let off at the trail between the two houses while Ned and Madge sat in the buggy, spooning. Knowing they would hear her, knowing Cora would hear her, hoping the people in Battle Creek would hear her, she had screamed, "Is he looking for a wife or a housemaid?"

Cora had been on the screened-in porch, ironing; she had stood leaning on the iron, speechless. Nothing had prepared her to believe that Sharon Rose had such resentment, such bitterness, in her. Cora had followed her into Fayrene's room, off the kitchen, seized her by the wrist, and whacked her palm with the back of a hairbrush, sharply. How well they knew what Sharon Rose thought of her hands! "That will teach you!" Cora cried, knowing that it wouldn't even as she said it. Not Sharon Rose. She had turned from Cora and run up the stairs.

"Mama," Madge had called, "now don't you cross

her. She don't mean it the way you hear it!"

In no world Cora cared to live in would she be so kind, so slow to take offense. In her soul she knew that Sharon Rose meant it even worse than she said it. She had come back from Lincoln hoping to share with Madge everything she had seen, and felt, and experienced, only to ride three in the seat of a buggy where she knew she wasn't wanted. The wild streak she had from her mother had made her cry out. Cora liked Ned Kibbee, and felt that Madge, a plain enough girl to look at, was fortunate to have him. What in heaven's name did Sharon Rose have in mind for Madge to do? Madge had no desire at all to waste time in school she could spend with Ned Kibbee. Was it envy? Was she possessive? Was it her pride that had been injured? Reasons were not lacking to explain such an outburst, but they did not satisfy Cora. In spite of her assurance that she had acted rightly, her cooling fury left her troubled. In Sharon's glance, when Cora had seized her, there had been less anger than pity. Pity for Cora, who felt no pity for herself. She leaned on the cabinet, propped on her spread arms, as Madge rattled the dipper in the water bucket.

"She likes Ned," Madge said. "She just don't like farmers," then she went off with the pail to the pump.

Whatever Madge had said, whatever she had meant, Cora's numbed, flickering awareness understood what she had implied. However much Sharon Rose disliked farmers, her scorn for farmers' wives was greater. She pitied Cora, who seemed to lack the sense to pity herself.

Ned and Madge were married in Olney, where he had his own people, then they came back to Cora's yard for the food and the reception. Under trees that Emerson had planted, on grass that had been freshly mowed that morning, they sat at picnic tables Ned had borrowed from the Burlington Railroad. During the eating and later the children played croquet with balls so new and bright they looked sticky. Ribbons were tied to the wickets as the lights dimmed, so the elderly wouldn't trip on them. Ned Kibbee wore the first pair of white flannel pants Cora had ever seen. There could surely be nothing more elegant and impractical. In the early dusk, candles were lit in the three sagging rows of Japanese lanterns. It made Cora almost dizzy to follow the zigzag flight of the bats. She would write to Sharon Rose, who had moved to Lincoln, that Ned Kibbee's relations were all upright people, three of whom had come from Sioux City, two with wives, to see him married. Other than what that implied, no admonishment. Sharon Rose would have to learn, by living her own life, that such losses were not easily recovered. From Omaha she sent Madge a comb and brush set in a velvet-lined case, the brush with silver backing, brushing Madge's hair being one of those things she really missed.

In August Sharon Rose visited her friend, Lillian Baumann, who lived just north of Chicago, in Waukegan. Most of the members of the Baumann family were musicians, and came together in the summer to make music. The Baumann house was so large that Mrs. Baumann was never sure how many rooms were occupied and who might come to breakfast. A huge lawn surrounded the house, with a garden at the back where music was played in an enchanting gazebo with a flag on the roof. Seeing it all from the window, Sharon Rose felt she must be staying in a fashionable resort. The Baumanns were so well-to-do it was hard to determine what they did for a living. Otto Baumann took the train to Chicago four mornings a week, being the head of a firm that made paints and varnishes. A picture of the firm's plant, on the Chicago River, with a water tank atop the building painted to resemble a can of paint, was on the wall of Mr. Baumann's study. The four Baumann sons had gone to school in the east, or worked in the east and lived there, but Lillian, the youngest of the three girls, went west just to do something different. One of her father's relations had settled in Lincoln, and that was why she came to Nebraska and not somewhere else.

Lillian was plain. Even in Lincoln she could spend a year and go almost unnoticed. Living with so many brothers for so long had satisfied her need for male companionship. She felt she had more to learn from an unusual young woman, like Sharon Rose. The young ladies had first met at the voice auditions, where Sharon Rose was the accompanist for Dr. Schumann. Lillian had come forward when her name was called and sung German lieder with such assurance that even Dr. Schumann had not checked on her voice. It was small, but she had such an easy presence it seemed much better than it was. Sharon Rose had style, and everybody said so, but her palms were moist before she sat down to play and even her listeners feared she might forget something. She was so petite. She was so cunning. How could she, Lillian asked, find room in her head for all that music? On occasion she didn't. She might go around and around and around, like a needle stuck in the groove of a record. She would do it with such aplomb, however, that her listener might feel it had been her intention. But not Lillian.

Even Sharon Rose was slow to see the style in Lillian's artless manner. Her figure had no lines of interest except for her remarkably relaxed posture. She wore strings of beads, which she cupped in one hand, the other hand placed at her hip in a way that was subtly provoking. Sharon remarked how the observer's glance returned to her face with renewed interest. Her best feature was a smile as elusive to read as Mona Lisa's. Was it mocking? It was often on her lips when Dr. Schumann praised her voice.

She had a *trained* voice, in Dr. Schumann's opinion, which he much preferred to an untrained voice. Her best moments were the solo bits in choral groups, where assurance and ease were pleasing as bird song. It was quite simply relaxing to hear Lillian sing.

The very opposite effect, to the point of discomfort, was the experience of listening to Sharon Rose. Although she was an accomplished young lady, her appeal was that of a *Wunderkind,* a prodigy. There were actually smaller pianists in the class, one of them a boy named Milton Sondschein, who could hardly reach the pedals, but the prodigious is seen on the mind's eye, and at the sight of Sharon Rose one had this sensation. Her specialty was Bach, the *Well-Tempered Clavier,* a source of pleasurable apprehension for Dr. Schumann, but the *pièce de résistance*—his own term—was her playing of the Partita in B-flat Major. Sublime music, of course, but one could not explain the special effects achieved by Sharon Rose. The listener who failed to chill, as at the onset of a fever, at the transport of the second movement, had no earthly business— Dr. Schumann's opinion—listening to music at all. In this appraisal he did not overlook the visual. Lillian Baumann had tried it both ways, with her eyes closed and with them open, but the fever of which Dr. Schumann spoke was more palpable with the eyes open. The spectacle of the *Wunderkind,* the conjuror, nimbly evoking the harmony of the spheres was crucial to the listener's impression, the notes ascending to a summit from where the descent was like that of a swoon. No, it was important that the listener sit alert, and not with tilted head, the eyes languorously lidded, an index finger steadying the head's tremor induced by the flood of emotion. Perhaps it was just as well, in Dr. Schumann's opinion, that Sharon Rose seemed to lack the performer's concentration; otherwise some entrepreneur would surely put her on exhibit, an experience so terrible that he erased it from both their minds.

Although ten years younger than her husband, Mrs. Baumann looked considerably older. She had never been robust, and after bearing and rearing seven children, she looked to Sharon Rose like a grandmother. Music had been her life; she had studied the harp, but given up performing when she married. That was not something she regretted, but a choice happily made. A tall woman, inches above the average, stooping to the concerns of her children had bent her back and rounded her shoulders. One could see by her eyes—usually averted from whomever she was facing, to check on something, or someone—how attractive she had been in her youth. On the death of her second son her hair had streaked with white. Something in her nature, in her tireless application, often led Sharon to think of Cora. The city of Chicago terrified Mrs. Baumann, and she was never at ease about her husband. While under her roof, none of her children were permitted to drive or own cars.

Through Mrs. Baumann's influence among musical people, Sharon received a scholarship to the Schurz Academy of Music on North Clark Street. She could have stayed with the Baumanns, commuting to the city, but she preferred to be more independent. In speaking to her mother Lillian used the word "freedom," which she seemed to prefer to the word "independent." One might say, and perhaps one of them did, that Lillian wanted her independence to be free, and Sharon her freedom to be independent. They agreed they would know a little better what they wanted, if and when they were deprived of it.

Several of the old homes near the academy had become dormitories for the music students, and Sharon could hear, until late in the evening, the muffled sound of the pianos on the floors below, although her windows were closed. Young men could be heard singing their scales in the showers. Strictly on her own, Sharon found part-time work as a clerk at the Newberry Library on Clark Street. This paid her nine dollars a week and made her financially independent. Her work was to return books to their places on the shelves, and she often found time to browse in several of them. Sharon liked to read novels, but occasionally they depressed her with the grimness of the life around her. This, in turn, might affect her concentration.

"Ware you are?" Madame Skaya would ask, rolling her eyes upward in a suggestive manner. But Sharon was never where Madame Skaya thought she was. If she was not doing the exercises she detested, infuriated by the tick of the metronome, she was in the studio of Miss Baden-Hall, working on the César Franck *Symphonic Variations.* Miss Baden-Hall gave her attention to scholarship pupils believed to show professional promise. She had known Brahms, Debussy, and César Franck, and once played four hands with Paderewski, whose technique at the time had been slipping. From her Lillian Baumann had picked up the taste for gray and black, with just a touch of white, and toying with beads while she lectured. Arthritis had shortened Miss Baden-Hall's career, and caused her to crouch over the keyboard, as if weeping. She had her own method of teaching. Her students would appear, take their seat at the piano, and begin to play with little assurance that the great lady was present. Sometimes she was not. This was all part of her method. Having the music in mind was nothing: one must have it in the heart. At that point where Sharon Rose's concentration often faltered (and they knew, how well they both knew!), Miss Baden-Hall would be there, smelling like a sprig of lilac, her hair brushing the flushed cheeks of the pupil, to repeat the passage correctly. No words were spoken. What did words have to do with music? Sharon Rose would be flooded with such emotion her eyes dimmed, and her heart pounded. It did not improve her playing, but surely it enlarged her capacity for feeling. The technique would come. First and foremost the artist must *feel.* It had been this, perhaps, that led Miss Baden-Hall to confront Sharon with the *Symphonic Variations,* music so committed to feeling that there was little else to master. Could it have been Miss Baden-Hall's purpose to disturb Sharon's remarkable composure? In that, certainly, she succeeded, although the cracks in her surface were hardly visible to others. Returning to her room, Sharon Rose might sit on the floor beside her bed like a sick child. She often felt drained of her proper nature. Her mind was like a liquid in a sloppy container. Her soul rolled from side to side of a rocking boat.

Lillian Baumann sensibly advised Sharon to get back to Bach and Mozart. Pure states of feeling, in Lillian's view, were not for this world. César Franck was as bad as or worse than Wagner in the way he led one on, eyes averted, from the wallowing pit of emotion. Lillian suggested the music of Scarlatti as a cleanser and a tonic, before she couldn't tell a mermaid from a Rhine maiden. Lillian was in voice, not the piano, but her experience with Mahler and Hugo Wolf led her to wonder if music wasn't the very devil's advocate. Lillian then confided, with the understanding that Sharon Rose would never breathe a word of it to her mother, that she had left the Schurz Academy and gone to Nebraska out of dread that she was *suffocating*. She couldn't put it better. She felt she simply lacked air to breathe.

Sharon Rose had never appeared so effortlessly composed as when she heard all of this on the beach at Waukegan, where they sat using each other as a backrest. Lillian had discovered this intimate way to talk and she also confessed that she found the very *idea* of marriage revolting, a barbarous arrangement for rearing and breeding. Look at her mother. Something that her father found it impossible to do. Not the demeaning captivity of marriage, but a free and independent sharing of life with a chosen companion. In England this was not uncommon. She went on to say that Miss Baden-Hall, who was English, had suggested that they spend the next summer in London together, but to be perfectly frank, Lillian found Miss Baden-Hall almost oppressive. The way she hovered about was revolting. It was not at all what Lillian would call a free and independent relationship. Sharon Rose, of course, knew this feeling so well, she knew it so *exactly,* that it brought on a fit of giggling, which left them both relaxed and carefree as children. Arm in arm they had walked along the beach until dark.

As they approached the house, Lillian had said, "There's no love among them. That's what I find intolerable." For just an instant Sharon had been puzzled. No love among whom? Fortunately, she didn't ask, and after thinking it over she knew exactly what Lillian meant. *They* were intolerable, all of them, their otherwise decent lives more like that of livestock than aspiring human beings. It both shamed and elated her to have such unthinkable thoughts.

The emotional swoon she experienced through her music was not entirely the doing of César Franck. Of course, Sharon had come east to visit Lillian Baumann, and study the piano with Miss Baden-Hall, but the reason she stayed and did not give in to homesickness had been Madge's decision to marry Ned Kibbee. Sharon had simply not believed that another person would take her place. With this shock there was the further revelation that women were incapable of binding friendships. They were willing to let men bag them like trophies. They gave no thought to the life they had rejected for the drab one they had chosen. They had been in Cora's garden, berry picking, and Sharon had stopped to fan the swarm of gnats from her face; without warning, Madge had said, "He asked me to marry him." That was all. Sharon had been too astonished to speak. All that same morning, and the previous night, Madge's thoughts had been on Ned Kibbee even as she laughed and chatted with Sharon. It mortified her to realize that in all their years together Madge had lived in *wait* for marriage. Still, it had not crossed Sharon's mind that Madge would accept him. She was like a calf, bred and fattened for the market, and the buyer had spoken for her. In Sharon's humiliation, the loss of Madge troubled her less than the ease with which Madge had surrendered Sharon. Now she had a husband. It more than made up for anything she had lost.

In the fall Fayrene had written to Sharon that Madge

was "thick with child," a repellent expression. There were many outrages, but surely none so distressing as one person's thoughtless rejection of another, no matter what the grounds. That woman should do it to woman, on the grounds that henceforth only the husband counted, testified to the truth of Lillian's assertion that women had been bred to be feeble-minded, and stay in their place. Sharon Rose took comfort in this point of view since it helped her to relate to Madge. She pitied her, but not in anger, as she pitied a woman like Cora.

It was strange how Sharon Rose, seated at the Baumann table, would find herself waiting for Madge to say grace. And if she used the bathroom, far down the dark hall, she missed having Madge with her. She had never been asked. She simply seemed to sense that Sharon feared the dark. Madge was the least nervous person in the world—a runaway team hardly got her excited—but while waiting in the dark for Sharon Rose she would break off the ends of twigs that were near her, a sound like someone stealthily approaching. Sharon Rose had been too ashamed to ask her to stop. It eased the silence of the night, and perhaps helped her ignore misgivings of her own. The two girls would then return to the house, Sharon's small hand gripping Madge's plump one, where they would pause on the porch to take sips from the water dipper. Fear of swallowing flies led them both to take little sips.

Madge closed all her letters to Sharon with the words "Mom and Dad are fine." It pleased Madge to think of them as sisters. If she spoke of Orion it was to say that he was not worse. Of Cora, Sharon had once said, "She cares more for her chickens than she does for us." She was not affectionate. She never handled the girls as tenderly as she did an egg. If there was affection in Cora's nature, it was not something she shared with people. Nevertheless, it was Cora Sharon thought of in moments of self-concern or self-appraisal. And yet just thinking about Cora might put her on edge. She could see her in her rocker with the wire-braced legs, nervously working her teeth as if gumming her food, fanning the air to her face with flips of her apron. Summer and winter, the living room glared with light. She sat facing this glare, as if blinded by it. Her remarkable face had no likeness for Sharon until she saw a book of paintings in the library. The intense staring eyes were those of icons. Insensitive to discomfort in herself, how was she to be open to it in others? In the suffocating heat she would say, "I like it better than the cold."

Sharon had sent Cora some Liberty prints from Marshall Field, suggesting that she make herself a dress or a blouse, then Madge had written to tell her that she had used the material for curtains. It maddened Sharon that she refused to think of her*self.* A box of English complexion soap she stored away in a drawer where the mice nibbled at it. Yet it was not lost on Sharon in how many ways they were alike. "Don't you two forget it," Cora had said to them both. "Your father and I have never been beholden."

It had seemed to Sharon, the first time she heard it,

a pitiful cause for pride. Now she felt different about it. It made no sense, for example, that Sharon could not accept Lillian's offer to spend the summer in England with her. Who would know that but herself? Lillian insisted. But that was just the trouble: Sharon Rose would know it. The independence Lillian had through money Sharon appropriated by being stubborn. She would not be beholden. How did that work out in matters of love?

Madge had written Sharon a long letter at Christmas (ignoring several months of silence) praising her husband, praising her life, eagerly looking forward to her *first* baby. Had it been necessary for her to say *first?* Her simple-minded goodness puzzled Sharon, yet it revived her affection for her. A few weeks later, on a piece of lined linen paper, given to her years before by Sharon, Cora wrote to say that Madge was "well," Ned Kibbee was "well," Emerson was "well," and she was "well." Only Orion seemed to be poorly. People were well if they were neither dead nor dying, unless so unwell they were "failing." The emotion Sharon Rose had in such abundance to lavish on her music would gather like a knot of pain in her soul.

The day following Lillian's departure for England, Sharon wired Madge (giving her quite a shock: a wire could only mean death in the family) that she was coming the following weekend. She had removed the word "home," knowing it was what all of them wanted to hear. She longed to see Madge, she wanted to see Cora, but a dread gripped her heart at the thought of what she might feel.

She had wondered if Ned Kibbee would recognize her, she had changed so much. "You've changed some," he said, but he did recognize her. She thought he looked older. A nail he had hammered had flipped up and struck near his eye, giving him a scar. The thought of it sent a shudder through Sharon, but he had merely mentioned it in passing. The news was that Orion was neither better nor worse.

Ned had stopped work on a house to drive to Columbus and get her, and he showed her the house as they drove by. She thought the frame looked small. He explained to her, as a builder of houses, how he often had trouble with the ladies because the frame looked so different than they imagined. The ground plan might appear no larger than a big garage. Some women almost wept when they saw the walls up, the house so small. Inside it seemed small until it had been plastered, and had something on the floor. Building houses he had come to know that, but he didn't know why.

While Sharon had been in Chicago, becoming a different person, Ned had built four houses with inside plumbing, their own cesspools, and furnaces in the basement. One of these houses had been for Madge. The reason it looked as bare as it did was that the trees and the shrubs were hardly started. When they pulled into the yard the wind lifted the sheets drying on the lines. Sharon's glimpse of Madge, her apron pockets weighted with clothespins, filled her with such emotion her eyes creased, and she thought she might bawl. She had a moment to collect herself as Madge walked around the sagging lines to get to her, a bonnet shading her face, the apron draping the bulge at her middle. Sharon babbled shrilly to relieve her feelings. Madge hugged and kissed her as she would a child.

"You can see I'm expecting again," she said. That was all. The baby, Blanche, was in the wicker clothes basket, in a heap of dried wash. Sharon thought the head was much too large for the body. The infant soberly returned Sharon's startled gaze. "They say she looks like Mama," Madge said. "Ned thinks so." And so she did. Already the large, deep-set eyes took Sharon's measure. The lips were firm. She would not smile until she was tickled. "I say she's like you," said Madge, "but I guess she's both."

"No Kibbee to speak of so far," said Ned.

"Cora says at least she's not born on a farm. She's got an inside toilet and running water."

Ned said, "You heard that one about the Indian?" Sharon hadn't. "This Indian goes to a hotel, for a room, and the clerk says he's got one with running water. The Indian doesn't want it. He says he wants a room all by himself." He moved his head from side to side, his eyes lidded. Madge allowed time for the joke to settle.

"Cora's well?" asked Sharon.

"She won't be happy till she's got her flush toilet," said Ned.

"She won't be happy then either," said Madge.

Ned propped the screen door open with the wicker basket as they squeezed by him into the house.

Ned Kibbee's mother had given the newlyweds a fourposter bed, made by her people in Pennsylvania; otherwise everything was new, inside and out. The fourposter bed was put in the guest room since it was difficult for Madge, once she was pregnant, to crawl in and out of it easily. It would be Sharon's bed as long as she cared to stay. Ned's mother and Madge had made the curtains, and all her friends in Battle Creek had given her a cuckoo clock which drove Ned crazy. If she was to use it at all, she had to stop it at night, then start it again when she got up in the morning.

The guest room had not been papered because the plaster had been so slow to dry. Now that it had finally dried, Ned didn't have the time. He had more work than he could do, but he had to do it himself if he wanted it done right. If the doors were hung wrong on a house they might never close right. Two boys had put the roofing paper on a house so that it looked as if the shingles were on edgewise. Madge had asked for, and got, a coal-oil stove, but once she had it she didn't like it. The wicks were always charred. The oil could be smelled all over the house. Smells she hadn't minded at all on the farm were disagreeable to her in the new house. The golden oak furniture had come so well crated Ned had used the wood to build a fruit cellar in the basement. The divan of the three-piece living room suite opened out to make a bed guests could sleep on. Madge found it hard to sit on, but not everybody had her short legs. Ned had put the same wax on the furniture that he put on the floor. To save the floor in the kitchen and the dining room, Madge had covered it with linoleum, which Blanche kept polished with the seat of her diapers. While Madge talked to Sharon, little Blanche nursed greedily. Sharon thought it unattractive in a baby girl. Yet it pleased Sharon to sit listening, and nodding, as Madge talked. In the past it was Madge who had listened to Sharon, mending what needed mending, or peeling what needed cooking, but no one would say to her now as in the past, "The cat got your tongue?" Madge missed her old friends, but it wouldn't be for long as the girls got married and the boys moved to the city. One of them had bought a lot just a block to the west. Ned would build him a house on it. He was sweet on Miriam Stoll. Did Sharon remember Miriam? She did not.

Madge had so much to say, while she was preparing supper, that she didn't get around to saying how much she missed Sharon Rose, although of course she did. During the meal, which Ned helped serve, it being tiring for Madge to get up and down from the table, she did ask Sharon what Chicago was like, and if Sharon meant to stay there. Sharon found a city so large was hard to describe. What she liked most was the lake, having never before seen so much water. She liked her work. In the library she often met interesting people. Lillian Baumann's home was like a resort, always noisy and alive with music-loving people. Had she made some new friends? Oh, yes, Sharon had made some new friends, including Professor Grunlich, on his sabbatical from Dartmouth, who liked to pause in his research to entertain Sharon with stories of his life in Paris, Florence, and other places. Professor

Grunlich would have liked to know Sharon better, but he feared to lose her by being too forward. He talked to her while she listened, nodding, returning books to the shelves. Madge would have loved to hear about Professor Grunlich, or even Orville Wiley, a young man she often saw on the Clark Street car in the morning, who kept a place for her by putting his hat and valise on the seat. He worked in the Loop, on La Salle Street, but he took drawing lessons at the art museum on Michigan Boulevard. He never tired of asking Sharon to go to the museum or a movie with him. She was always too busy. She did not like the way he took the liberty of calling her Puss. Madge would have very much liked to hear of these friends, but Sharon was reluctant to bring them up. What Madge wanted to hear was not about her friends, unless they were boys. What was it in Sharon that refused to give Madge, who had every right to know, this small satisfaction? For her part, Madge found it hard to imagine getting up and going off every morning, or living in a place with so many people she would never know.

On Sunday Ned drove them all out to the farm. From the road at the front the house looked about the same, with the paint scaling on the exposed side. After more than twenty years Emerson had given up thinking of putting on a front porch nobody would ever use. Everybody came in and out at the back. Down at the end of the driveway the barns and sheds were the faded color of bricks, the cottonwoods at the back taller and greener than Sharon remembered. Emerson now milked a herd of eighteen cows. It was worth the trouble of a Battle Creek merchant to come to the farm twice a month for Cora's butter and eggs. Almost a hundred fifty chickens, most of them now Leghorns, laid their eggs where only Cora knew where to find them, but Orion was around to help her clean them and put them into cases made for just eggs. Until the car wheeled around to face the house Sharon had forgotten about Cora's yard, the grass clipped as short as the lawns in Chicago. A quilting frame with an unfinished quilt was set up in the shade near the back porch. A few old hens pecked around in the dishwater scum near the screen. The shed to the west, the original house, had been painted green with white windows; the cobs inside pressed against the glass. A covey of pale-gray doves sat on the dung-whitened ridge of the shingle roof. There was no sound but their mournful crooning. Was it the absence of people? Sharon could not account for the way it moved her. Cora's weathered house—one defined it as Cora's —a square frame house with screen-dulled windows, seemed to Sharon, as she approached it, charged with disturbing expectations. The trail that edged the grass, from the porch to the pump, was hard and smooth as old boards. Her nose to the screen, Sharon saw Emerson's hats on the range food warmer, beside his tin of Union Leader tobacco. On the table near the door the dipper floated on a full bucket of water. The draft off the kitchen smelled of scorched ironing. The screen was latched.

"Call her," said Madge. "See if she knows you."

Huskily Sharon said, "Oh, Cora—"

"She won't hear that," said Madge, and gave a rap on the screen. Until she moved, Cora had been invisible. She rose from the cot in the room off the kitchen, which had appeared to be empty.

"It's so warped," she said aloud, referring to the screen, "I have to hook it against the flies." She unhooked it, then allowed her gaze to rest on Sharon. On the stove, simmering, the lid of a pot wobbled. Cora said, "Lord, child, you've grown."

"It's the heels, Mama," Madge explained.

They faced each other without touching. To Sharon, the lath-flat, graying woman looked taller. Did she move back a step to see Sharon better, or to maintain her distance?

"Aren't you surprised?" said Madge. Ned stood behind her, holding Blanche.

Cora said, "You might have called me."

"I'm not used yet to your having a phone, Mama."

"Let me take her," said Cora, and reached to take the sleeping child from Ned. "One of you go wake Emerson," she said.

"Oh, don't wake him," said Sharon. "Let him nap."

"How you expect him to see you if you don't wake him?" Cora moved before them, saying, "Come in here where it's cool."

"If we wanted it cool we'd stay in the yard," said Madge, "but we don't like the flies." Gnats buzzed in the halo of light caught in her veil. "I'm dying of thirst," Madge said, rattling the dipper. "It's got so I'm already used to ice."

Cora said, "If you'd have phoned I'd have thought

of something." She led them through the dark dining room, the blinds drawn, into the glare of the front room.

"What do you see that's new?" asked Madge. The three women stood together at the room's center. Sharon peered around.

"The rug," she said. The rug was new. The old rug had worn away beneath the rocker.

"What else?" asked Madge.

The piano was not new but it held Sharon's attention. The player rolls were stacked in even rows along the top, the labeled ends exposed. An open hymnbook sat on the rack.

"You're too citified," said Madge, and tilted her head to look at the ceiling. A bulb hung there on a cord, with a paper shade. Madge reached forward to give a tug on the dangling cord. The bulb glowed with a visible tremor.

"It does that when the motor's running," said Ned, "not when it's off."

Madge said, "I still don't believe it."

"We don't need it in the daytime," said Cora, and switched it off.

"There's something else," said Madge, giving Sharon a wink, "but oftener than not I forget it."

Cora made no comment as Sharon turned to look at the telephone on the wall. The wallpaper was scuffed and soiled where their knuckles had rubbed it turning the crank.

"Can you believe it?" asked Madge.

"It just comes to me," said Ned, "it's up too high on

the wall for Sharon to use it." He stood at the door to the kitchen, his face perspiring, holding a dripping dipper of water.

Cora said, "Which one of you is going to tell Emerson he's got visitors?"

Sharon would later tell Lillian just how it was she felt, but not what she saw. Cora had taken a seat in the rocker, holding Blanche, the brim of the blue velvet bonnet turned back from her face. The lids of her eyes opened and closed to the rhythm of Cora's rocking, like those of a doll. Cora appeared to be gazing into her own face as an infant. A clumping sound caused the light bulb to wobble as Emerson descended the stairs. At the kitchen door, the light in his face, his eyes were pale as water; his sleep-tousled hair rose to a wispy peak. Seeing Sharon, he said, "So you come back?"

"She's on a visit," Madge replied. "She's on a visit."

Sharon said, "How are you, Uncle Emerson?"

"He's better now he's give up chewing," said Cora. "It was chewing gave him the weight in his stomach."

"I sleep better too," he said, "except for the times people wake me up."

It startled Sharon to see how mild he looked. In her childhood he had been such a heavy presence she had seldom looked at him directly. It was the top of his balding head she saw when they said grace. Ned brought them all glasses of water in amber-colored glasses.

"You took her company glasses," said Madge.

"They're for iced tea mostly," said Cora.

"They make it look like iced tea, but it don't taste it," said Emerson.

Sharon said, "Chicago water is terrible. You can taste and smell the chlorine in it."

"Now, why they do a thing like that?"

"They take the water from the lake, and they do it to kill the germs."

There was silence, while Emerson pondered what he had heard. Putting his right hand to his jaw, he stroked it as if feeling for a sore place, the beard making a rasping sound.

"I've never felt drawn to cities," said Cora.

"Ella-noise is prairie country," said Emerson, "flat as a pancake."

Madge said, "Where'd you read that?"

He was immune to sarcasm.

"Ned," said Madge, "you better get Orion."

"If he's restin', let him be," said Emerson. "It's what he does best."

Sharon said, "How is he?"

"He's well as you might expect," Cora replied.

Through the curtained window at the side they watched Ned follow the trail to Orion's house. Sunlight dappled the roof and the sheets of paper on the floor of the outbilly. Cora offered Blanche one of her knuckles to chew on, removed it and said, "She's cutting teeth already." Emerson adjusted the movable back of the chair so he could sit upright.

"This chair was worth every nickel it cost me," he said.

"It didn't cost you a nickel. Orion gave it to you."

"That's what I said."

"How's Fayrene?" asked Sharon.

"She's with her people in Okie. She pays them a visit every summer."

"She's got a boy sweet on her," said Emerson.

Madge said, "You don't know sweet from sour."

"I know a boy from a girl," he replied, "and I'm beginning to wonder if I've seen the last one."

Cora said, "They'd all be boys if it was up to me."

She rocked, her gaze through the door to the shimmer of light rising from the road. Sharon wondered if she had forgotten the child in her lap. The screen to Orion's house slammed, then they could hear the swish and crackle of the branches as the men came toward them. Sharon saw him, in advance of Ned, cross the yard with his hurried, almost stumbling stride. He wore his hat to conceal the whiteness of his head. What were her feelings, besides sorrow and pity? She had never been at ease with her father. He was the neighbor who came and went. He smelled of liniment. Now he came headlong through the kitchen to where the light and the assembly stopped him, his hands lifting slowly to frame his face. His eyes blinked. He seemed to have trouble focusing. The man she saw was no farmer but a city bum, like those idlers in the parks of Chicago, his clothes wrinkled with sleep, his pants grass-stained at the knees.

Cora said, "Sharon's here on a visit." She continued to rock, without turning to face him. He had come over so fast it left him winded, wheezing. His head and his hands trembled. Either he didn't see Sharon clearly, or he seemed to doubt what it was he saw. She had forgotten how the inside of his lips showed red when his jaw hung slack, or he mouthed a cigar.

"She looks like her," he blurted. It startled them all.

"Like who?" asked Madge.

His head wagging, he said, "Her mother."

Emerson said, "I don't remember her standin' still long enough to be seen."

"Maybe he saw her," said Cora, wetting her lips, "like he knew he wouldn't have her long to look at." In the silence the child in her lap whimpered, putting a fist to one closed eye.

"It's past her time," said Madge. "I best be getting her home."

Cora said, "Fayrene's not going to like it she missed you."

Orion moved from the door to let Madge, Cora, and Sharon pass through the kitchen. Emerson stayed in his chair. Ned went ahead to hold open the screen. When Sharon glanced back from the yard, Orion stood on the porch, his head tilted back, taking large gulping swallows from the dipper. This impression of Orion, his Adam's apple pumping, would replace all the others Sharon had of her father: a man greedily drinking as if unable to quench his thirst. As they drove along the driveway to the road, she saw the light blink on in Cora's kitchen. "You see that?" said Madge. "She'd never do that if we was still there."

To Sharon, Ned said, "How they look? They look about the same?"

"Orion's slipping," said Madge. "He's forgetful. He'd forget to eat if Cora didn't call him. But it did her good to see you. You're like one of her own."

When Sharon had left the farm to live in Lincoln, she had emerged from an oppression so habitual she had hardly suspected its existence. On returning she sensed her submergence to that lower level of feeling. As if drowsy with ether, she observed their movements and listened to their voices. Did this partially conscious life offer comforts she would live to miss? Half consciously she sensed that. The physical presence of Madge, thick with another child, reduced Sharon's capacity to think, blurring the line between the young woman who recently departed and the one who had returned.

Each day of her visit Sharon put off till the next day asking Madge how she liked marriage. It seemed obvious. How imagine her in another context? Each day after lunch, they sat in the shade cast by the house, with Blanche in the wicker basket between them. The child never cried. She resigned herself to lying on her back rather than her tummy. She resigned herself to Madge's attentions; she resigned herself to Sharon's indifference. Sharon was not too fond of children, and Blanche had resigned herself to that.

"I suppose you like city living better?" Madge asked. A film of moisture gave a shine to her plump face. She had pinned up her hair to feel the coolness of the draft on her neck. It startled Sharon to realize that she would like the city better if Madge lived in it.

She could see her with Blanche on the grass in Lincoln Park, or on a bench at the zoo.

A doctor in Columbus had told Madge that she had too many teeth in her lower jaw. It amused Madge to learn that. It gave Sharon dull shooting pains in her teeth. When they had been little girls it was often Sharon who knew that Madge was sick before Madge did. There were veins like those in a leaf at the back of her knees.

There might still be light in the sky when Ned Kibbee went to bed. He would water the lawn while they washed and stacked the dishes, coming in with his shoes soaked by the wet grass. Sharon would hear the alarm go off at five-thirty, and the pad of Madge's feet as she walked to the kitchen. At night they might sit up, after stacking the dishes, and listen to John McCormack on Madge's new Victrola. Madge had sung for three years in the Battle Creek choir, and liked a good tenor voice. She did not have a musical gift herself, but she felt a gift for it ran in the family. It had turned up in Sharon. There was a touch of it in Fayrene. She came back from the Ozarks with her neck and arms tanned, but her face still a botch of pimples. Madge always hoped she would come back different than she went away. Fayrene was a slender, shy girl, with pigeon breasts so high they looked artificial. At the sight of Sharon she had been speechless. The boy sweet on her, Avery Dickel, had a good job in a creamery in the Ozarks. Fayrene was being encouraged to practice on the flute for the Battle Creek band.

There were spells when the two women said nothing they remembered, or were aware that they had said. Ned Kibbee helped himself to the food on the table that Sharon no longer took the trouble to offer. He didn't think it rude. He really preferred to help himself. Without interrupting what she was saying to Sharon, Madge would spoon-feed food into the mouth of Blanche, half of which she spat out. While eating she tightly clenched her little fists and banged them hard on the shelf of the highchair. Madge's comment was that like her daddy, she would make a good carpenter.

Ned took time from his work to drive them both to the station, where Madge refused to weigh herself on the waiting room scales. "It's no business but my own," she said to Ned. Ned weighed 179½. Sharon weighed 104, including one pound of homemade fudge. She would come to visit them again at Christmas, if she cared to, or if not at Christmas, early the next summer. Hugging Sharon to her the best she could, Madge repeated, "It did Cora good to see you. You're like one of her own."

The long night of fitful sleep on the train Sharon felt herself in limbo, neither coming nor going, seized with a longing that had no object. What was it she wanted? Loneliness overwhelmed her. The lights of villages flashing at the window, even the glow of lamps in solitary farmhouses, made a mockery of her independence. What was it in her nature that led her to choose a life alone? If the man across the aisle, graying at the temples, reminding her of Professor Grunlich of Dartmouth, wearing a Palm Beach suit with bits of grass in the pants cuffs, buckskin shoes with toes that were grass stained—if this man had spoken to Sharon, if he had suggested she join him for dinner in the diner, if he had sensed, as he surely would, the contradictory needs in her nature and had been free to administer to them, the Sharon Rose who boarded the train in Columbus might not have been the one who got off it in Chicago, and the book of her life might have been different. But he did not speak to her. When she awoke from a spell of napping he was gone.

During the Sunday service Madge studied with interest every married couple she could set her eyes on. There they sat. A few hours earlier, there they lay. Some on their sides, some on their backs, and a few on top of each other. She saw it only dimly, but as something she had experienced she could accept it. It strained her mind, however, it strained her very soul, to accept this fact for the others. The women corseted and solemn. The men sober as judges. Between and beside them the children that had to be made.

Madge would soon have been married for sixteen months. Was there a day of fifteen of those months she had not pondered her experience? Wanting children, she had been prepared for the worst, knowing that the worst had happened to Cora. It could be endured because it need not happen too many times. Madge had chosen Ned as a man she liked and had felt he might minimize the necessary torment. This proved to be true. It had startled her to find how such an easygoing man could become, on the instant, almost a different person, but this could as soon be said of herself. It more than startled her to admit it. She was humbled and bewildered to find that such a torment gave her pleasure.

What would her husband think if he knew that she enjoyed it? Her pains to deceive him relaxed when it seemed clear that it hardly mattered. She had assumed it would end with her pregnancy and was part of a new bride's remarkable sensations, but with the child born she had felt desire for her husband. That she concealed, of course, scarcely admitting it to herself. She had no way of knowing if Ned was aware of her reluctant-willing collaboration. She feared what might happen if she took the initiative. Now that she was pregnant again he turned on his side and was usually snoring while she brushed her hair. She liked his snoring. What would it be like to have a man who lay snoreless and awake?

Madge had hoped that Sharon had come back to say that she had met a man and planned to get married. Only when this had happened would Madge be free to hint that she found Ned different than she had expected. In what way? Sharon would ask. Madge could not touch on it until Sharon had had the experience. The two girls were open and frank with each other, but they had seldom discussed men and boys. They had never discussed boys and girls. Sharon had blurted out her opinion of marriage on hearing that Madge was engaged to Ned, but Madge felt that this was in part her anger at losing her friend. Sharon was such a pretty thing, like a beautiful doll, Madge found it hard to see her sleeping with a man. She was like a child. How did such little women mate with grown men and have babies? Madge was curious. She felt in Sharon no curiosity on the subject. Madge had had a baby. It might have been brought by storks.

That this baby was a female, the image of Cora, the fifth girl child in a family of females, might have discouraged a man like Ned from the prospect of a large family. Of Mrs. Kibbee's five children, three were sons. The two girls, who came third and fifth, had the advantage of a likeness to their mother, a handsome Scotswoman with almost orange-colored hair and a complexion she had to keep out of the sun. The two daughters were married off before the sons, one to a station agent in Fremont. Mrs. Kibbee felt that children blessed a marriage, but not if they ran exclusively to girls men did not consider attractive. Mrs. Kibbee spoke to Madge, feeling that the woman had the final say in such matters, and Madge was grateful for the advice, knowing that it was so well intended and being in agreement that a family of girls you couldn't marry off was hardly a blessing to a marriage. Madge didn't say so, of course, but to have borne Cora's child as her first one had led her to look forward to the second, her first child being, in everything but name, Cora Atkins's second. Anybody could see it. Nor was it Madge's nature to deceive herself. Some weeks before Mrs. Kibbee discussed the matter with her, Madge was two months pregnant with her second child, not a word on the subject of children having been exchanged with her husband. Need there have been? He would have left it to her. He was like Emerson in the way he would walk and stand at the screen if she had a problem, and hear what she had to say while he gazed at the sky and picked at his teeth.

"You do as you see fit," he'd say, and push the screen open to close the discussion. With a hammer, a saw, and some nails he could build a house, he could measure, consider, and come to decisions, but all matters that he couldn't hammer, saw, and measure he left to her. She was flattered.

"Ned takes care of the outside," she said to Sharon. "He leaves the inside to me." Weeks after Sharon had left she found herself pondering what she had said. It did not please her that Cora might have said the same thing.

"She looks like her father," Cora said of Madge, "but she's not at all like him. She likes to work."

She was slow, and she took her work easy, as she had to, but she liked it. She differed from Cora. Unfinished work weighed so on Cora's mind she might get up at night, or from a nap, to do it. Told to rest, she would reply, "I can't rest while there's work to be done." In that very fact Madge took pleasure. Leaving off at night, or resting during the day, she thought of the unfinished ironing and mending and fruit canning. That it remained to be done reassured her. That it was endless did not depress her. She got up pleased in the knowledge there was work to be done. Ned had bought her a motor-driven washing machine that spared her the drudgery of tub-washing sheets and diapers, but she reserved his shirts and socks for the pleasure it gave her to use the washboard. She liked the sound of it. She liked the feel of it under her knuckles. A new bar of Fels-Naphtha soap seemed as fragrant to her as bread from the oven. She liked to slice it as she did butter. The smell of soap on her hands was not unpleasant. The laundry chore to which she looked eagerly forward was hanging out the wash: the blue-whiteness of sheets stretched on the line, and their sun-dried sweetness when she took them by the armful and squeezed the fragrance into her face. They smelled to her like freshly kneaded dough, or cooling bread. Ironing she kept for evenings, when it was cooler, her board set up in the draft from the back to the front, her skirts pinned up so that it would blow cool on her legs. In the winter, the side blinds drawn, she would take off her dress and iron in her slip, her backside warmed by the hot air from the floor radiator. The glide of the iron, the silken feel of the cloth, the sight and smell of a new scorched patch on the pad (reminding her of Cora) were overlapping pleasures so satisfying she delayed work that she might have finished. While ironing she reviewed the day's events, or lack of events, reflections that might come to her mind at a time when she was not in a position to enjoy them. The scorched odor of the pad was attractive to her, and like strokes of the iron, her mind would pass over and over the wrinkle in her thought till she had smoothed it out. Tilting the iron on its end often signaled a resolution, and the slap of her moistened fingers on its bottom, testing its heat, indicated a fresh beginning. Her own swelling body had its scent which puffed from the dress she stretched on a hanger. She liked to iron without her slippers, enjoying the coolness of the linoleum floor in the summer, and the warmth in the winter, the pipes of the hot-air furnace passing beneath. Ned browsed in the catalogues while she ironed, comparing Ward and Sears Roebuck prices, smearing the heel of his hand with the order forms he had made out with his indelible pencil. She was a help to him in wording letters of complaint.

Cooking was a chore that had to be done, but it gave Madge little satisfaction, eating being a chore necessary in the performance of duty. Ned ate without comment, his head over his plate, glancing up to look for something that proved missing: Madge read these glances and handed him the salt, the sugar, the syrup, the butter. She had her own breakfast later, when her hands were free. He was fond of his pancakes hot from the griddle, two at a time. She liked to watch him eat. Watching him eat she first saw his long tangled eyelashes. As well as she knew him she wouldn't think of mentioning it. Every man she knew smoked, or chewed, or both, but Ned did neither. "How come you don't smoke or chew?" she had asked him, the first thing she had liked about him. "I guess I never started up," he replied. As a carpenter he needed his mouth free to hold nails. He hammered one thumbnail so many times it surprised her it wasn't black. She said to him, "Ned, you got just one pair of hands. You go on like this and you'll have just a half pair." He startled her by replying, "Which half you like me to pinch you with?" Actually, it wasn't so unlike him to pinch her, but it was not at all like him to say so. If he caught her stooping he might give her rump a slap, or give a flip to her skirts as she passed the table. "Ned Kibbee!" she would say. "What if your mother saw you?" "She prob'ly did," he replied. "She don't miss much." Most people were ignorant of the playful side to his nature. Sunday afternoons he would lie on the floor and let Blanche crawl over him looking for his head. He could hide it so well the child would get worried. Playing with her father was the only time she smiled. He could give her hiccups by lowering his head and blowing his hot breath on her belly. "What's she going to think if you keep that up?" Madge joshed him. "She's going to like boys more than girls," he replied.

Nothing more than that was ever said between them on a subject that went unmentioned. Until Ned had made the comment, Madge had had no idea that he was aware she might have options. Did he know what they were? How had he concealed from her such thoughts as he had? She knew so well what he would say before he spoke up this other Ned Kibbee aroused and disturbed her. What might he be thinking? Did he think about all of the things that she did? The way they slept together was acceptable to Madge because it took place in the dark, and required no discussion, but her very consciousness quivered to think that he thought about it in the light of day. When he lifted his eyes to glance at her, might it be on his mind? This alerted her to feeling that she possessed, at the root of her nature, something that she should not surrender, and it was a lucky thing for them both that she felt this the keenest when seven months pregnant. So there was no occasion for her to show reluctance where she had been such a willing accomplice.

The winter was a bad one, with the snow drifting to conceal the windows on one side of the house, so that she had to keep the lights burning, and sometimes woke up at night feeling that they had been buried alive. The silence terrified her. She would have to get up and rattle pans around in her kitchen, shivering in the heat from the oven. Ned slept so soundly he didn't miss her. A month before the child was born she decided on the name of Caroline, if it was another girl, or Raymond if it happened to be a boy, choosing it in the hope that a name like Ray would make a boy's life easier. In Madge's judgment, her Uncle Orion had suffered most of his life from the name he'd been given, requiring that people ask him to repeat it and boys his own age make fun of it. Nor had the name Emerson helped her father, a man too solemn to be given a nickname. Only Cora could pronounce it so often and not grow to hate it. Long before she learned

that the name Beulah was a common one among col-
ored people, Madge had grown to dislike it. Fay, Ray,
Bess, Les—names that came easily to the tongue were
the ones she liked. But Ned had his Aunt Blanche, a
favorite, and his sister Caroline Louise, who would
look on the new child with more interest if it had her
name, and didn't look like Cora. Madge would like a
boy for Ned, but she really didn't mind having girls for
herself. They would be a help later, and little girls
could grow to mean, as she knew, a great deal to each
other. Madge could already sense that Blanche would
need someone like Sharon to like her, and she would
never get from an aggressive little boy what she just
might get from her sister. They should be as unalike
as Madge and Sharon Rose.

In February Fayrene came in from the farm to help
around the house while Madge had her baby. Madge
was not quite three years older than Fayrene, but she
sometimes felt she could be her mother. What was it
that held her up? Fayrene was a willing worker, but
Madge was always surprised to find her a good one. If
it was something she baked, Madge checked the oven;
if it was something she mended, Madge checked the
garment. "It wasn't Cora who taught you to mend like
that, was it?" Madge said. "No," she replied. If Madge
wanted to know who it was that had taught her, she
would have to ask her, "Well, then, who was it?" Four
out of five times it would be Mrs. Cullen, the wife of
the pastor in Battle Creek. Madge and Sharon Rose
hardly knew her to speak to, yet she had taught Fay-
rene most of what she knew. That could only mean

that Madge and Sharon Rose had been like Siamese twins, as Emerson described them, and gave no thought to Fayrene. Had she stood and watched them? Had Madge or Sharon ever said, "Where's Fayrene?" She had her own room in the house, right off the kitchen, where Cora called "Fayrrrrrr-een!" as if she lived with Orion. Being so much alone should have made her independent, but instead it made her shy and quiet. Madge could be in a room and fail to notice Fayrene was there. Her bad complexion came on her right at the time she was about to meet boys and get around a little, but the only one she knew worked in the creamery in the Ozarks. He wouldn't lack for girls if it crossed his mind he ought to get married.

Fayrene came into the house on February 8 and on the eleventh Madge had her second child, a chubby, almost blond girl with the close-set eyes of the Kibbees. The birth was not so easy for Madge as the first one, and Dr. Maas recommended—since she had Fayrene to help her—that she stay off her feet and rest for a spell. Madge was strong, but her legs gave her trouble if she spent, as she did, most of the day on her feet. She was a little top-heavy, in Dr. Maas's opinion, and the time she spent at the sink or the ironing board put a strain on her back and knees. If she meant to go on having children—and Dr. Maas took that for granted —she would need to reduce some of the house chores that put a strain on her legs. Dr. Maas was the first to point out to Madge what a strange sort of creature people were in the first place, women especially, obliged to live as they did standing upright, and not down on all fours like most animals. Madge had never heard talk like that before, and Dr. Maas let her draw her own conclusions. He was a gruff man, with his own problems (his rheumatism was so bad he winced when he shook a thermometer). Madge sometimes detected an unusual odor on his breath. With Fayrene in the house it was possible for Madge to spend more time sitting, but she found it boring. It was her nature to get up and do it herself rather than ask somebody else to do it. One trouble with Dr. Maas's suggestion was that Fayrene was best at cooking but hardly to be trusted with ironing. She couldn't seem to get the knack of ironing the collar of a shirt, or keeping the heat of the iron right for a sheet. She was sweet and patient with Blanche, however, careful with dishes, and like one of Ned's own sisters. She had learned from Cora that something well mended was better than ever. A hole never reappeared where Cora had mended a sock.

Cora's new phone line was down during part of February but she called Madge on Washington's birthday to see if it was back in operation. She had nothing in particular to say, but she did it in a voice that indicated she lacked confidence in the apparatus. Madge used the occasion to talk over with Cora if in the last few weeks she had missed Fayrene. Cora did not especially miss her, but she felt that Emerson and Orion did. Emerson complained about her every day of his life but now that she was away he was restive. She wasn't there to play checkers with him. Orion missed her at meals. Madge said it wouldn't only be a help to her but better for Fayrene to live in Norfork, where there were more boys and girls her own age and a high school she could walk to. Cora said at her age she ought to be old enough to know her own mind.

Fayrene's own mind told her she would miss everybody—Aunt Cora, Uncle Emerson, Orion, and Blossom, the horse she rode to school when the weather permitted—but she liked living in Norfork, taking care of Blanche, and having her own money. Besides her room and keep, Madge would pay her five dollars a month. That was three dollars more than she had made helping Cora sort her eggs for market, four dollars more than she had made helping Emerson shell his popcorn, and two dollars more than Madge had made when she was her age.

It wasn't necessary for Madge to get up when Ned did, but she would rather do it than lie there awake, listening to the noises in the kitchen. As soon as Ned was out of the house she could go back to bed. With Fayrene taking care of Blanche, Madge could give her attention to little Caroline. The child loved to be fondled. If Madge brought her face up close and blinked her eyes, Caroline would gurgle and squirm with delight. Right off the bat the child knew men from women and was a regular flirt with her father. People do like to fondle a chubby, cunning, soft blond baby, rather than a dark, sober, angular, bony, unsmiling child. They were both Madge's girls, but Caroline got most of her attention, and when she didn't get it she was quick to complain. Madge couldn't punish the child for what she had brought on herself. What she had not foreseen was that a baby so small could be so jealous. If Ned put her down and picked up Blanche she would have a tantrum. That amused Ned, but it led Madge to wonder if it might not lead to trouble. Of all the things she didn't want in this world it was a spoiled child. It pleased Ned to see how little Caroline would put on a show to win his favor, but he was puzzled and irritated when Madge couldn't stop her whining later. Ned would never believe, nor would Madge bring it up, that a child who couldn't talk could play one of them off against the other. And when she began to see it, it was too late. There was no way she could put pressure on Caroline that was not a concession to her, so that she got her father, or she got her mother, in every showdown with Blanche. No one would believe —how believe in an impression so fleeting—that a child exchanged with its mother a glance of cunning and triumph, as Madge stooped to provide her with what she asked for, or idly fingered the buttons of her blouse. The solemn Blanche would sit there silent, eyeing them both.

The two babies looked so strange together—like similar creatures from different litters, one blond and chubby, the other dark and lean—that Madge let Fayrene push Blanche around in the carriage while she carried Caroline. That way the contrast was not so great.

"Do you like one more than the other?" Ned asked her. This startled her. Was he observing and wondering? She had never imagined he would be that curious.

"I suppose I give the new one more attention," she replied, not wanting to reveal more of her feelings.

Would that prove to be true of the *next* one? "At least I know what not to do next time," she said, it pleasing him to hear she was once more pregnant, but it troubled him to hear what she was saying. Madge had given little Caroline more attention, in part because she knew how to demand it, but with her pregnancy she was aware that she gave less of herself than previously. Already she was holding something in reserve for the new child. If Sharon had been with her she might have confessed that it was knowing that that made Caroline so demanding. But Sharon would not have been curious. It had displeased her to learn that most of the weight Madge had put on was not her own.

In June Fayrene went to visit her folks in the Ozarks, and for her own sake Madge hoped she would stay there. If the creamery boy asked her to marry him, that's what she should do. She discussed this with Cora on the day she took the babies out to see their grandparents. In Fayrene's former room, off the kitchen, Orion had installed a water closet, but the bowl wouldn't flush until he got a water tank on the roof. Over Emerson's objection that electric bulbs would upset the chickens and cut down on their laying, Orion had put lights in both of Cora's henhouses, at the door to the cobhouse, and on a pole at the pump. Emerson said it wasn't a farm anymore, but a Christmas tree. He might have had lights instead of lanterns in his barn, but he feared the cows wouldn't like it; if they took a dislike to something it cut down on their milk. Rural electrification was coming to some counties but Emerson wasn't sure he wanted that either, now that (thanks to Orion) they had their own generator. The less Emerson had to do with government people the better he liked it.

It was unusual for Emerson to talk so much, but he seemed to take a shine to little Caroline, even though she was a girl. Watching him bounce the child on his knee, Madge remembered he had once done the same with her.

> "Clipety clop
> Clip-e-ty clop
> She can't walk but
> She sure can hop!"

He was a comic with the babies, but a solemn owl with everybody else. "Let's see this one here," he said, picking up Blanche, but the singing and the bouncing didn't amuse her. Her head would rock from side to side but her eyes never left Emerson's face. He confessed to Fayrene it gave him the willies. "Gimme the other one," he would say to Madge, and pass Blanche, her legs dangling, to Orion. Caroline would squirm and howl if given to Orion, but Blanche would sit picking at the white dog hairs on his blue serge suit. If he made her a face, or blew smoke through his nose, she would watch but never squeal or laugh. In a joshing tone Emerson would say, "That one come with a tongue?" and tickle her in the ribs. Blanche would squirm but she wouldn't giggle. When Madge asked Dr. Maas if Blanche shouldn't be talking, the look he gave her was that she should count her blessings, with Caroline more than ready to talk for them both. It amused Madge the way Ned liked to fondle Caroline but was taken with Blanche, her owl-eyed silence and sober gaze appealing to something unspoken between them. Ned liked it, but it got on Madge's nerves. So much went into her mouth, and so little came out. The alarm clock on Ned's side of the bed would sometimes not run unless he banged it, and the God's truth was that was sometimes how Madge felt about Blanche. If her head hadn't been so wobbly on her neck, she would have given her a shake.

Fayrene came back from the Ozarks two weeks early, with an itchy rash on her arms and backside. It spread to wherever she scratched herself, and proved to be poison oak. Madge had never seen anything spread so fast and look so horrible. They called in Dr. Maas to prescribe for her, and he took Ned aside for a consultation. As unlikely as it seemed, he said, it looked to him like Fayrene was pregnant. Did she know any boys? Here in Norfork she didn't, nor men for that matter, but it was known she was friendly with this boy in the Ozarks, who worked at a creamery in Okie. Well, Dr. Maas said, to both Madge and Ned, she didn't get what she's got from a water fountain. This boy she knew, Avery Dickel by name, was the son of people who were friends with her mother, Ned said, and he took the weekend off to drive to Missouri and speak to them. They didn't believe it either, but when the boy was asked he admitted to it. His parents agreed with Ned that the sooner they made their vows the better, so he came along with Ned on the drive back. He was not just the person Madge would have chosen, but she was distracted by his joshing manner, as if he didn't know what he had done. Even with the worst over, Fayrene looked so bad Madge couldn't believe she would ever look normal. Her hair had to be cut off while her scalp healed. As a child Madge had wondered what a leper looked like, and now she knew. Avery Dickel himself kidded about her appearance the way he would a dog clipped for the summer. It was probably this quality in Avery that led Fayrene to be so fond of him, as well as his indifference to how she looked. Madge went to great pains not to give Sharon the impression that the marriage was sudden and uncalled for, emphasizing the fact that the poison oak led them to put it off until Sharon could pay them a visit. After all, she *was* her sister, however hard it was for either of them to believe.

Before Lillian Baumann returned from England in September, Madge called long-distance to tell Sharon that Orion had just had a stroke; he couldn't talk, but for him that was not too much of a loss. Mostly, she was calling for Fayrene, who was to be married while she was recovering from poison oak, and at this time in her life, her daddy with a stroke, it would comfort her to see her own sister, her closest next of kin. Sharon was actually so flustered by the long-distance call she agreed to what she heard to keep the call short. Hours later, sleepless, she realized that Madge had known just what she was doing. She knew that Sharon found Fayrene depressing, with her terrible acne and painful shyness. Nevertheless, Sharon knew she would go, rather than not be there when Cora cried out, "Where is Sharon Rose?"

After a long night in the coach seat, where she huddled like a child, half draped with the topcoat of the conductor, what Sharon saw through the soot-smeared window was like a continent under water. There had been heavy rains; deep ruts fouled the roads, water sat in pools that reflected the sunrise. A sway-backed white horse stood like a specter in a field of corn stubble, its head drooped as if too heavy to support. The dip and rise of the telephone lines, which she had once found so distracting, seemed wearisome and monotonous to her, like the click of the rails. It might have been an abandoned country. Even the towns seemed curiously vacant. It seemed incomprehensible to Sharon that people continued to live in such places. Numbed by the cold, drugged by the heat and the chores, they were more like beasts of the field than people. Where a lamp glowed a woman like Cora would be lighting a fire, setting a table, or gripping the cold handle of a pump, the water rising with the sound of a creature gagged. Only work that could not be finished gave purpose to life.

At the station Ned Kibbee came forward to greet her, flecks of his breakfast at the corners of his mouth. He said, "You have a nice trip?" and carried her bag to a car with side curtains. He avoided her glance, but she felt his pride in the car. Bundles of shingles were piled in the rear seat. "She's a good girl," he said, when the motor turned over, "but there's times she's a slow starter."

"Are cars girls?" Sharon asked. "Why is it a she?"

Ned hadn't thought about it. He appeared to be thinking while he was driving, but he didn't speak. Sharon had never given thought to it herself, but it seemed a good question once it had been asked. "I don't see a girl as a motorcar," she said. "Do you?"

"You'd see it different if you were a man," said Ned, and he looked to Sharon for confirmation. The hairy back of the hand he rested on the gearshift was powdered with sawdust the color of corn meal. How different would Sharon see it all if she were a man? She felt a knot of evasion at the center of this casual, seemingly sensible answer. It would have pleased and reassured Madge; why did it displease Sharon?

Ned had spread a bed of gravel over part of the yard, where he parked the car. At the back, work had started on a garage with a peaked roof. A boy, wearing a Sherwin-Williams paint hat, stopped pounding nails to gawk at Sharon. A railing had been added to the porch at the back of the house. At the screen, his shirtsleeves rolled, stood a young man who filled the doorway.

"That's him," said Ned to Sharon. "That's Avery."

Avery Dickel, the young man sweet on Fayrene, opened the screen door to let them in. Sharon was either so pretty, so small, or both, that he blocked the door and stared at her, his jaw slack. "You never seen a pretty city girl before?" Ned kidded him, and it seemed Avery hadn't. Madge cried out, "Will you men let her in?" and they moved to one side. She was on her feet, her hands braced on a chair back, to give support to her swollen figure. "We'll need a larger house," she said, "if I get any bigger, won't we, Ned?" Ned nodded his head that he thought so. Madge was too big now for the girls to hug each other, but she stooped enough for Sharon to kiss her. A smear of pancake flour whitened one cheek. "This is Avery," she said, "Fayrene's beau. There's no bed in the house long enough for him. It's a bed Ned has to build them before he does a house!" Avery Dickel flushed the color of Dentyne gum. The feverish color whitened the fuzz on his beardless cheeks. A more oafish youth Sharon had never seen, but he was too undeveloped to be ugly. He had not said a word. Madge said, "Where's Fayrene?" and turned to look for her. Fayrene was at the stove in the kitchen. A barber had clipped her neck at the back, but her hair was in curlers. The sleeves of a new pink robe were turned back on her freckled arms. Sharon saw her face, dimly, through a blue cloud of bacon smoke. "Heavens amighty!" cried Madge. "You let him see you burn bacon like that?"

Fayrene was speechless. They stood together watching her burn the bacon. "Open that window behind her," said Madge, "to help air it out."

She went ahead of Sharon, her apron strings dangling, to rinse the sawdust off the soap in the bathroom. "I can't get him to rinse his hands first," she said, and sorted out the towels to find Sharon a dry

one. Her head wagging, she added, "We've been wait-
ing for this to happen," and sighed with relief. There
was nothing of the misgiving, the disbelief, the dis-
may, that Sharon had felt at the sight of Avery Dickel.
"They can live in Orion's place," she went on. "Fay-
rene doesn't mind at all taking care of her daddy. It's
going to help her to have a place of her own. She's
going to make a good wife."

There wasn't room for them all at the kitchen table,
so they sat in the dining room, flooded with sunlight.
Madge spoon-fed Blanche, who sat with her eyes wide,
her mouth closed. In order to breathe, Avery Dickel
kept his mouth open as he chewed. In profile, Sharon
could see that his teeth grew forward, like those of an
animal meant to crop grass. It shamed her to feel that
something Avery couldn't help would lead her to find
him so unattractive. The way he stared at her, as he
chewed, upset her less than his unawareness that she
was gazing at him.

"Avery works in a creamery," said Madge, "but he
don't like it."

Fayrene said, "He's going to be an animal doctor."

"A veter-nary," said Avery.

Ned said, "That's good business if you stay clear of
the dogs and cats."

"Farm animals a specialty," said Avery. He stopped
eating to enjoy their attention, suck air between his
spaced teeth. The sound he made was like that made
by Ned when he called the Kibbee cat, Moses, to come
and eat or be scratched. A blue Maltese with the tip of
his tail gone, Moses went slowly around the table to

look up at Avery, who reached down to stroke him, then scoop him up. With a practiced gesture he curled back the cat's lips, showing his yellow teeth, and using the thumbnail of his right hand, he chipped off flakes of tartar like scales of paint. "See that!" he said, holding the thumb toward Sharon. She was too stunned to react. "They get like that," he went on, and drew the hand back to look at the chipped particles more closely. Sharon thought she might be sick, and closed her eyes.

"Animals like him," said Fayrene. Amazingly, the cat did seem to like him. If Ned or Madge had scraped at its teeth they would have been clawed. Avery cleaned his thumbnail on the edge of his chair seat and peered across at Sharon, whose mouth stood open. Was he checking *her* teeth?

Madge said, "Something like that might take time, won't it, Ned? Until they're settled they can live on the farm."

Ned said, "You needn't farm it, just live on it."

"Orion did well with his pigs," said Madge. "If you like animals you can just raise pigs."

"I don't mind pigs," replied Avery, "but I don't like 'em."

"He don't like chickens either," said Fayrene.

"You won't need any chickens," said Madge, "if you just look for the eggs laid by Cora's Leghorns. She don't trouble to look for more than she needs now."

The scraps of food from Avery's plate Fayrene scraped onto her own, as she stacked the dishes.

"Let people finish," said Madge. "You begin like

that, it's going to be hard for you to stop, you hear me?"

Ned winked at Sharon, said, "I don't plan to get married, so I better get to work. I got work to do." Sharon stared at him so intently she saw the pupils of his eyes expand, then contract. A fine meal of sawdust powdered his lashes, the creases of the lids. As he arose he took the last swallow of his coffee, walked with the cup and saucer to the sink.

"You let Avery do that," said Madge, "and you'll never have a meal in peace." She pushed herself back from the table, tilted forward to rise. "You two sit and get acquainted," she said to Sharon. "There's no need for you to help."

Avery leaned on the table, his tongue probing for food above the gumline. In that manner he had of being self-unaware, he stared at Sharon, his head tilted like the dog on the horn of the Victrola. His cheeks were like apples. A snow of dandruff powdered his shoulders. In all her life Sharon could not remember a young man, or a young woman, she found so repugnant. In a mocking tone she asked, "Would you like to be a farmer?"

"I like animals," he replied. It had not yet crossed his mind to say that animals liked him.

"Then you'd just love farming," she said, "since everybody on the farm is an animal. It just takes a little time." He was silent. Did it mean he was pondering what she had said? In the effort of concentration his brows twitched, his right ear wiggled. "I suppose my problem is," she went on, "that I don't really like animals enough. I like people better. I don't think they should resemble animals."

What had come over her? What she had said, however, now that it had been said, seemed so obvious she was pleased to have said it.

"What's so wrong with animals, miss?" he asked.

His calling her "miss" disarmed her. Alone with him, she had been apprehensive he would use her name, as if he knew her.

"Nothing's wrong with *them,*" she said, rising from the table, flushed by what she heard herself saying. He gazed at her with wide-eyed wonder.

"You go take a nap," said Madge. "There'll be plenty of time to talk later."

"Excuse me," Sharon said, and walked through the house to the room at the front, with its unmade bed, the cuckoo clock on the wall to the left of the bureau. It had stopped with the bird popped out of the house, at ten minutes to five.

For a woman so young, Madge moved around like a grazing cow. She heaved herself out of chairs, eased down with a whooshing sigh, propped herself on her arms at the sink or the table, and yet these effortful movements seemed to increase her contentment. She oozed creature comfort. She smelled like a pail of warm milk or sheets dampened for ironing. Unable to stoop, and no room left to her lap, she let Sharon attend to Blanche.

Babies intimidated Sharon, especially this one. She could not rid herself of the impression that her limbs suspended from her head, like a spider's. Scary or comical faces, loud or strange noises, balloons, dancing lights, or even the water sprinkler (placed on her head so that it sprayed all around her), did not disturb her solemn composure. How like Sharon that was! Sphinx-like, little Blanche would fasten her eyes on Sharon and follow each move, like a bird on a perch. Sharon could feel the child's gaze on the back of her head. The largeness of the head and the thinness of her neck caused her head to lob and roll, as if it might twist off. She had an amazing pallor, disturbing to Madge, but promising a cool, marble-like complexion. Nevertheless, Sharon found it hard to burp the child or change her diapers.

Would her baby sister encourage Blanche to talk? Ned thought so, but Madge didn't. When she was ready to talk she would. The unflinching steadiness of her gaze was not like that of a child at all. How did one know, Sharon asked herself, if such a thing was exceptional or retarded? Babies her own age Blanche sat aloof from and stared at. Did she like music? She pounded with her little fists on plates, pans, and the shelf of her highchair. Da-da-da! she sang. But a performer more than a listener. Cora had found and repaired an old rag doll of Madge's cut from a pattern in a Ceresota flour sack, but Blanche had showed little interest in it. That spoke to Sharon. Did this child look about her and find all of them strange? A creature destined, perhaps, to be a stilt-legged beanpole, like Cora, among these contentedly grazing heifers, excelling at the spelldown, the falldown, and the Music Memory Contest. Few boys would press against her at the turn of the stairs. In her highchair at the table, on a level with Sharon, she might avert her gaze in such a manner that she spied on Sharon through a tangle of lashes while grace was being said.

"Say it again," Madge said. "I don't think everybody heard it." Fayrene's voice was little more than a whisper.

"Bless this food to our use, and us to thy service."

"I never tire of hearing that," said Madge. "It's why I eat so much."

On their way to the farm they went through Battle Creek to visit with Mrs. Eichelberger, their former teacher. She had been the one to insist that Sharon continue her music. Had she continued? she asked. Yes, Sharon had continued. Mrs. Eichelberger proved to be more at her ease with Fayrene, whose job had been to collect and clean the erasers. Did Avery Dickel know she was such a good speller? Not much of a speller himself, he hadn't noticed. Fayrene was hardly talkative, but if asked questions about her plans to set up housekeeping, she would answer. One of the rewards of teaching, Mrs. Eichelberger said, was to see the coming of the new generation, with girls like Fayrene to excel at spelling, and boys like Avery to pelt them with snowballs. How much like their parents they often proved to be! If they settled on a farm, their children would go to school in Battle Creek. Mrs. Eichelberger looked from Avery to Fayrene, then back to Avery, slack-jawed as he listened, Mrs. Eichelberger pleased at the prospect of children who would prove to be the image of their parents. Her expression did not change when she turned to Sharon and asked if she expected to remain in Chicago, or come back and settle down.

Madge walked beside Ned, with Blanche straddling her hip, peering solemnly back at Sharon. Fayrene had run on ahead to the car to make sure she got a seat without the side curtains. As she ran, Avery pelted her with green crab apples. When Madge stooped to pry a bit of gravel from her shoe, her immense backside was like a hamper of washing. Ned gave her a pat, as he would the rump of a horse.

The autumn day was beautiful, rows of shocked corn standing in tepees in the warm, diffused light, but Sharon did not feel her customary pleasure. What image did Madge have of Sharon if she saw Avery Dickel as a member of the family, related by marriage to all of them? Admittedly, Fayrene had to do what she could, and Avery Dickel might make a fine husband, but neither Madge nor Ned had exchanged with Sharon a knowing glance. Avery was no longer an Ozark hick and a hillbilly Dickel; he was Fayrene's beau and that made him all right.

So that Orion could look on, from his wheelchair, the wedding was held in Cora's front room, the shades half drawn against the road glare. The light bulb seemed to crown Avery's head. Sharon stood with friends of Fayrene—Lura and Mabel—within the sound and smell of jars boiling on the range. Cora had tomatoes waiting to be canned as soon as the newly-weds departed. When Sharon had greeted Orion, his popped eyes open wide, Cora had said, "He can hear you, but he can't talk back." Hearing that, he had audibly whimpered. From his head she had removed his black hat, stroked back his hair, then returned it like a pot cover. A confusion of sorrow and pity numbed Sharon to what she was observing. The broad back of Madge blocked her view of Fayrene; the air smelled sourly of Caroline's wet diaper. When they all turned to look for Sharon their perspiring faces beamed with relief. Something had been done that could not be undone, as long as life, as binding as death. Later Emerson would say, "With a name like that you'd better have girls, so they can change it." Fayrene hugged and kissed him. Had she heard what he said?

"We often wondered who Fayrene would marry," Cora said, with no indication of what sort of person she found him.

"Ma'am," Avery replied, "with me right there next door, you can see for yourself!"

At the north edge of town Ned pulled off the road to tinker with the carburetor. Sharon sat as if drugged. Flies hovered over Madge as she fanned them away from the faces of the children. As a drowsing child, seated in the church pew, her ears ringing with the voice of Cora, Sharon sometimes confused who and where she was with the words and images of the hymn they were singing. Until she knew better, "Brighten the corner, where you are," had been "Right in the corner, where you are," which she found somewhat puzzling but appealing. How well that seemed to describe her state of mind. The heat drone of the insects, the stupor of the food, and the jostle of the car seemed to blur the distinction between herself and the swarming life around her. Voices, bird calls, a movement of the leaves, the first hint of coolness in the air, were not separately observed sensations but commingled parts of her own nature. Her soul (what else could it be?) experienced a sense of liberation in its loss of self. What she admired in Cora, yet disliked in Emerson and Avery Dickel, was that they were less persons than pieces of nature, closely related to cows and chickens, and Sharon Rose, for all her awareness, blew on the wind with the dust and pollen that made her sneeze.

Madge and Ned both insisted that Ned drive her to Columbus to catch the train. On the long ride down, Ned was more talkative than usual. Sharon gathered that it had been planned by Madge so she and Ned could be alone together. Above the crunch and rattle of the road gravel he told her how relieved they were to get Fayrene married, although it would work a hardship on Madge with a new baby coming. Ned did not say so, but with Fayrene married, that left only Sharon. Did she remember Arthur Willard? She did not. Well, he had been just one year ahead of her in school, which meant that he may have looked down on her at the time. He was now settled in Norfork, in his father's law practice, where Ned often saw him on business matters. He always asked about Sharon Rose. In particular he always asked if she was yet married. Madge would tell Sharon, if she was asked, that Arthur was the pick of the local bachelors. He was on the short side, but so was Sharon. This trip was not the time to bring it up, but Arthur Willard had expressed the desire to meet her. The next time she made a visit they would do this. Arthur Willard had already discussed with Ned the sort of house he would build, once he met the right girl. There was nothing they could put in a house in Chicago that Ned couldn't put in a house in Norfork, Lincoln, or any place Sharon might like better. The one thing that Madge wanted was to have Sharon close by somewhere. "Don't she run nice!" he said, relieved to have it over, to have done what he could to settle her future.

He boarded the train with her, and she felt his assurance that she was leaving only in order to hurry back. The conductor was advised to keep an eye on her; the porter was paid in advance for her pillow. When the train began to move she felt an inexpressible relief. The clang of the last crossing bell rang down the curtain on ceaseless humiliations, inadmissible longings, the perpetual chores and smoldering furies, the rites and kinships with half-conscious people so friendly and decent it shamed her to dislike them.

"This seat free, miss?" The young man stood in the aisle, hovering above her. As tall, perhaps, but not so oafish as Avery. Clutched to his front he held a fiber laundry carton, tied up with a cord. He took her silence for assent, dropped his bundle in the seat. "I'll be right back," he said. At the back of his head, as he walked away, clipper nicks exposed snippets of his bone-white scalp. A moment later, his eyes glistening, he came toward her with a paper cup of water; it spilled on the seat as he passed it to her. Leaning to the window, he rubbed a clear spot on the glass with the heel of his hand, but the film of dirt was on the outside. "It's up ahead," he said. "We're coming to it."

"What is?" she asked.

"Colby," he replied. "I'm from there." Sharon would remember his reflection in the window, his eyes moving as he searched the darkness. "Look there!" he cried. She saw nothing but his reflection. "Boy, am I glad to see the last of that!" he said, happy in his freedom, in his expectations that whatever life held for him in the future, it would henceforth be his own life, it would not be the life of Battle Creek or Colby, it would not be the trauma of birth or burial, or mindless attachments to persons and places, to kinships, longings, crossing bells, the arc of streetlights, or the featureless faces on station platforms, all of which would recede into the past, into the darkness—wouldn't it?

In August of 1933, assured that it would last until they got there, Ned Kibbee drove Madge, Cora, and the girls to the World's Fair in Chicago. For a week or so Cora's chickens would have to see to themselves. Emerson had no desire to go to a fair that he was told had neither cows, pigs, nor draft horses. Not that it mattered, since there wasn't room for him in the car, and he wasn't asked.

Cora sat in the rear, gripping one of the posts that held up the top. The side curtain with cracked isinglass windows cut down on the wind, but flapped like a shade. Words spoken by Madge, intended for Cora, blew away like bits of paper. The tongue Cora put to her lips, a lifelong habit, caused them to dry and crack. Fences and poles, furrow after furrow, field after field, farm after farm, flashed past. Her eyes watered. The unaccustomed jostling, the wind and racket in her ears, the loss of appetite and the increase of thirst, the smell of Blanche's buttered popcorn and Caroline's cream soda, proved to be a greater strain on Cora than her trip west with Emerson, which had taken twelve days. At thirteen, Blanche was taller than her mother, with a spinal curvature that needed correction. Her eyes were like lanterns, the skin of the lids stretched taut and translucent to conceal them. She was very much a problem in the public washrooms. Ned had to stop the car near a grove of trees where Madge or Cora could take a walk with her. Cora had ceased to be disturbed by Blanche's silence once it had been proved that she could talk. She was quick to understand what Cora said, and did not pester her with foolish questions. All by herself Blanche had learned what Cora had never managed to teach her sister— where to look for eggs. It also pleased Cora to be told that it was from her the child had her flawless complexion. Other ways in which she knew they were alike she kept to herself.

Why would a woman who had lived her life with outdoor accommodations take exception to the indoors of a gas station toilet? Shame at what they might think discouraged her from going into the woods with Blanche. There was a difference in farm dirt, dirty as it was, and city filth. The farm dirt was her own. Seated on the stool in a rented room, Cora could do nothing whatsoever but sit there. All of her functions had stopped. With averted eyes she heard Madge say, "Mama, if you can't do anything, you tell me." So little her own flesh and blood knew her as to say that.

They found rooms in a boardinghouse near the fairgrounds, from where they could walk across railroad tracks to the entrance, but Cora spent all of the first morning alone, in bed. Her head throbbed with the noise below the window. In the evening, Madge washed what the girls had soiled at the fair, standing with her back to Cora, talking. Ned had to help her into the corset from which she bulged at the top and bottom. Cora had never seen so much of her exposed. Above the sound of running water she confessed to Cora that she had been advised not to have another baby. Cora had no choice but to hear it. Not to see it, she closed her eyes. Madge went on to say that Ned wanted a boy, as she did, but there was no guarantee that she would have one, what with nothing but girls in the Atkins family. Another girl she did not want. Look at the ones she had. Blanche had reached the seventh grade because the seats in the lower grades were too small for her. She would not do exercises, salute the flag, or arithmetic beyond fractions. Caroline was so bright she frightened people, and already, in the sixth grade, she was boy crazy. All Madge could say was thank God for poor little Rosalene. Sucking her thumb, which nothing would stop, had proved to be a blessing and kept her quiet. She did as she was told. If her complexion didn't sunburn, she would make some farm boy a nice wife.

Never before had Madge talked to Cora so openly. Being in a strange place had unsettled her, as it had all of them. Cora gazed at the windows, where the light glared, her emotions confused. She hoped to minimize what she heard by saying nothing herself, keeping her eyes averted. Madge hung the clothes she had washed and rinsed on the iron frame of the bed. Where had she learned that? It seemed to relieve her to speak in this manner to her mother, and shuffle around in her stocking feet and her corset. Cora did not understand it, but she sensed it to be a compliment.

Rosalene and Caroline came back from the fair with blistered heels. A coolie hat had sheltered all of Blanche but her insteps, which were sunburned. Ned had bought Rosalene a yo-yo and Blanche a live chameleon she wore like a pin on her blouse. Cora saw its colors alter when it was placed on the carpet. Later it was lost, then found, high in the fold of a curtain where nobody could reach it. All but Cora went with Ned to eat hot dogs, one of which they brought her, with a bottle of root beer. She had thirst, but no desire for food. During the night she woke thinking the chameleon was in her bed. The lights of beacons crisscrossed on the sky, and what she thought to be the moon proved to be a balloon descending. Late as it was she could hear music, and the sound of revelers. It dazzled her to think, as Ned had told her, that the fair covered more ground than Norfork, some of it on an island of rocks built into the lake. Lights came and went, but at no time did the room grow dark. Above the half-lowered window of the bathroom she watched the sky light up before sunrise, the street below her littered with papers that fluttered about like chickens. If asked at that time she would have said that she had seen everything.

Yet it left her unprepared for the bedlam of the fair itself. Weary and dazzled, she sat with Rosalene on a bench near where music was playing. The players were on a stage, the sun glinting on their instruments. It differed from anything she had heard in the way it soothed and calmed her.

In one of the vast exhibitions, so tired she was dazed, Cora sat with the girls for a photograph. Over them arched an arbor, with painted flowers and birds. The thought of a true human likeness is miraculous, but the picture itself is even stranger. The scene is dark, but there she sits, like a stuffed owl. Perhaps she had no idea what she looked like. A tight line seals her pleated lips. Caroline squealed with laughter when she saw it, but Blanche pressed her hands to her cheeks as if to widen her eyes, her lower lip held fast by her teeth. The pin at Cora's throat reflects the light, wisps of hair appear to be lines in her face. As the ears have grown larger, the head appears to be shrinking. Unquestionably it is Cora, but it is also an image that defies grasping. Madge puts it away to look at it later. Cora will never see it again. What she saw was so bizarre it left no afterimage. However briefly she had seen this "likeness" it changed the substance of her nature. She was no longer the person she had been, but something more or less.

Later that day they watched the fireworks until the air had cooled and Madge could put her shoes back on. Ned said that Cora was asleep before her head hit the pillow, but she was awakened by claps of thunder and flashes of lightning. The curtains puffed like sails until Madge closed the windows. In the morning Caroline found Blanche's chameleon under the covers at the foot of Cora's bed, a piece of its tail broken off.

Cora and Madge had planned for weeks to meet with Sharon Rose on the last day of their visit. Ned would take the girls to the zoo in Lincoln Park, and Madge, Cora, and Sharon Rose would have lunch in the pavilion, where they could talk. At the very last moment, while Ned was parking the car, Cora was possessed by something. She could hear the shrill piercing voice of Sharon, and feel the rage in her body, like that of a trapped animal, when Cora had whacked her palm with the hairbrush. "That will teach you!" she had cried, but what had it taught her? When Ned appeared she flatly refused to go along with Madge. "Mama, you sick?" Madge asked her, and maybe she was. As if she couldn't bear to do it alone, Madge took Rosalene along with her. Caroline and Blanche went along with their father, leaving Cora free to sit on a bench facing the animal cages. Ned bought the girls balloons they asked Cora to hold. Seated alone, in this throng of people, Cora was seized with a sadness so great her throat pained her. Madge didn't like the way she looked when she came back to her, and they drove to the lakefront, where it was cooler. Ned parked where they could look at the water. So much of it, endless and calm, soothed Cora, the color deep as a bluing rinse, her gaze fastened on the smoke of a boat beyond the horizon. Madge said that Sharon Rose was fine, prettier than ever, and still doing her music.

They drove back through the Dells, in Wisconsin, where Ned took them all for a boat ride. Cora sat at the front where the oars wouldn't splash her. It frightened her to look deep into the clear water. Rising to leave the boat, one hand extended toward Madge, Cora became confused, the boat tilted, and she toppled, her arms flung wide, into weeds and shallow water. She was pulled from the lake like a drenched fowl, spread to dry in the sun. Her left hip seemed strained. The twisting fall had wrenched her back. Ned drove from the Dells to the farm without stopping, Cora propped bolt upright between him and Madge. Long after sundown they reached the farm, the pits scratched by the chickens visible in the car lights. The noise and commotion stirred up the hens, but did not disturb Emerson. Because of her lameness Cora was put on the cot off the kitchen, propped up by pillows. Ten days later she was still there, but able to move around with the support of a chair, gripping the back. It broke her lifelong habit of being first person up and down the stairs. When she was able to climb the steps if she cared to, she had grown accustomed to the cot off the kitchen, and to sleeping propped up. Emerson made no comment. As he had all his life, first thing in the morning he drank a dipper of water without skimming off the flies. What was left in the dipper he tossed through the screen, which caused it to rust.

More than five years after Orion's death Sharon reexperienced her troubled sense of loss as suppressed feelings of guilt. She neither liked nor disliked her father. She felt detached from and indifferent to him. Perhaps she rather hoped it would be possible for her to overlook him. Like an infection that had failed to localize, her feelings of guilt had been slow to surface. When he came back from the war, however, it had shamed her to feel only pity for him. For Fayrene she felt a distressed compassion since she seemed doomed to complicate her misfortunes, but she was aware that her attitude toward Blanche had changed.

Sharon marveled at, rather than pitied, the gangly puppet-limbed child with elbows that appeared to bend inward at the slightest pressure, or when she clasped her hands behind her back. She was now trapped in a school with oafish boys and giggling girls, where she was moved from class to class, from desk to desk, to accommodate her ungainly figure, her still growing legs. She was leaner and more cranelike than Cora, with the matchless complexion her father thought to be unhealthy. Sharon could not help staring at the pearly lobes of her ears, the shell-like transparency of the wings of her nose. If a lighted candle could be placed in her mouth, would she glow with an inner light? Yet she seemed as at ease in her environment as she looked out of place. She could not learn fractions. She had no interest in civics or history. While these subjects were under discussion she made her childlike drawings of animals and birds. Her teacher, Miss Ringle, had been relieved to find she could entertain herself and not prove to be a problem.

At home Blanche was the darling of her father and the object of Caroline's relentless taunting. She made beds, and sat for hours attentive to little Rosalene's prattle. Was it any wonder that she was silent? Any impulse to speak was reserved for her father, who put his finger to her lips to spare her the trouble. Sharon sensed that it embarrassed him to confront a girl child who was taller than he was. He thought it enough, by way of communication, to blink his eyes in such a manner it led her to shyly lower the lids on her own. That's what she had always done as a child, and she was still his child. Put out to Mrs. Ord, to learn piano, she had not progressed beyond "Chopsticks." Was there possibly a problem with her hearing? What business was it of Sharon's?

Sharon could no longer bear the thought, nor avoid it, that this girl child would soon appeal to some loutish youth stimulated by the seasonal fall of pollen, and be thick with child. The thought almost sickened her. In a family of girls one sacrifice (Fayrene's) was enough. Before the cocoon of Blanche's childhood had peeled away she would be locked into the trap that nature and man had set for her.

Hadn't Madge repeatedly said that what Blanche needed the most was an older sister the likes of Sharon? (Rosalene had such a companion in Blanche, silent though she was.) With a directness that would appeal to Ned (she had to be tactful) she would write to Madge suggesting that Blanche might attend this school for girls in Waukegan, since there was simply nothing further for her in Norfork. She would spend her weekends with Sharon. The Briarcliffe School, which Lillian had attended, made allowances for young ladies who were unusual or gifted in the manner of Blanche. These things were on Sharon's mind when she heard from Madge (such coincidences were not unusual between them) wondering if Blanche might pay her a visit (it was early July), since with school out, and all the girls at home, Caroline was almost too much for them, especially Blanche. Rosalene would fight her back and shriek at her, but Caroline couldn't resist heckling a person like Blanche. Nor could Madge plan to go off to the Ozarks, or somewhere else, without them. All winter Ned had had his heart set on going to the Black Hills, where he hoped to do some fishing, but the girls would simply not allow him a moment to himself. Blanche would not be going on to the new junior high school but would help Fayrene with her newest baby. She was so patient with babies it was too bad she didn't have one of her own.

If Madge had not closed with that remark Sharon might have done no more than think it over. Instead she wrote to say yes, yes she would be glad to, if the time could be arranged before her own vacation on the Cape in August, never dreaming that when that time came she would cunningly contrive, like a kidnapper, to take Blanche along with her, rather than spend the weeks at the sea without her, brooding on her exile and waste in Norfork.

Sharon was not inexperienced in the far reaches of friendship, and infatuation, but nothing had prepared her for the great pleasure she received from Blanche's mute passive presence, her undemanding yet constant attention. Her beauty was certainly peculiar, as pronounced and unusual as something imagined (not at all lifelike), recalling the women seen in the paintings of the early Flemish and Dutch masters, so self-contained, so unrealistic they aroused no further expectations. To contemplate their appearance was more than enough.

Within a week of her arrival Sharon had begun her

connivance to keep her. In this, the situation in Norfolk played into her hands. From the Black Hills Madge wrote her to say what a great relief it was to be free of the haggling girls. Caroline herself had changed now that she received all of her father's attention. As for Ned, not having a son, a tomboy like Caroline secretly pleased him. The two of them shot at bottles with an air gun. After a letter like this Sharon took the steps she had contemplated but feared to acknowledge. It was the declared purpose of the Briarcliffe School to accommodate the exceptional student, even when the student seemed markedly disadvantaged. The principal, Miss Holroyd, one of the founders of coeducation in England, had only to set her eyes on Blanche to exchange knowing glances with Sharon. Of course! Who would ever know what might flower on such a branch? Nor would it be hard, with so many to choose from (they came to Briarcliffe from all over the world), to find a suitable roommate. Sharon did not trust herself to write a letter, so she called Madge on the phone—pleading the need of a quick decision, to ensure her place in the school—closing the conversation with Blanche, herself, speaking softly but clearly to her father. Yes, she was happy. Yes, she looked forward to going to school. That in itself was so unusual no further discussion proved to be necessary. Blanche would come home for Christmas and spring vacation, but other, shorter holidays she would spend with Sharon, including most of her weekends. It all went so well Sharon overlooked the remarkable change in Blanche. How account for her assurance?

Reflecting on this transformation, Sharon thought back to the private decisions of her own childhood, when she had felt her nature threatened, culminating in the moment she had filled her lungs and shrieked to the intruder seated in the buggy with Madge. A force she was born with. One that would go off when it was tapped.

Blanche's roommate, a plump, thick-calfed girl named Shirley Caudwell, a hockey player from Charlottesville, Virginia, had the chronic cheerful nature of fat children and loved to eat. She received food parcels from her family weekly, as if they feared she might starve. Tinned meats, preserved fruits, baked Southern hams, baskets of fruit given to voyagers on shipboard. She shared it with her classmates, but to Sharon's dismay little of it clung to the limbs of Blanche. Eating so preoccupied Shirley that Blanche's reserve went unnoticed. Two weeks after her arrival Blanche did seem to experience a brief spell of withdrawal, thought to be homesickness, but it was hard to distinguish in a girl like Blanche her normal retired nature from an abnormal reaction. The activities of the art department, under Mademoiselle Arnaud, a Belgian woman, so preoccupied Blanche that her day proved to be too short. She was *slow*. There was little or nothing said, however simple, that she did not have to have repeated. The projection of slides, the collecting of art prints, the mounting of prints on varicolored papers, the drawing of plaster-cast hands and heads, in charcoal, on papers of assorted colors and textures, all of this in a room lit up by a skylight under trees flaming with fall colors. Blanche wandered about in her bibbed green smock, her fingers ink-stained, her cheeks smeared with chalk dust, the marks of her sharp pointed teeth flaking the enamel from her drawing pencils. None of this long concealed from Mademoiselle Arnaud her unusual nature and remarkable beauty. Blanche was also content to sit for her portrait —something quite beyond the talents of the others— leaning forward, her chin resting on her hand, or comfortably slouched, her legs folded beneath her, the light falling in such a manner her skin was transparent as porcelain. That was quite beyond the students to capture, of course, but Mademoiselle Arnaud, who did watercolors, and knew exactly how to use the cream tones of the paper, in some of her quick sketches captured Blanche's serene detachment. It was quite uncanny in a girl in her early teens. Equally arresting was to observe Blanche when she was shown these portraits of herself. Most girls, their emotions confused, would giggle, or feel embarrassed to shamelessly stare at their own likenesses, but Blanche would soberly ponder these images as if they were portraits of someone else. One was used as a frontispiece for the yearbook—a portrait to please most Briarcliffe parents— and Sharon often found Blanche shamelessly gazing at it, as if pondering its meaning. There seemed to be so little vanity in this recognition Sharon did not speak to her about it. It might have been another person, understood to bear her a close resemblance.

In addition to her art, surprising Sharon, she also proved adept at botany, where she became a specimen collector, the sill of her bedroom window jammed with bottles of bugs and growing seeds. Blanche pressed leaves well, made excellent pressings and rubbings, but persisted in her chronically bad spelling and reversal of the letter *S*. When this was pointed out she was very attentive, and could make the correction recommended. The following day she would revert to the one she liked. However puzzling, Miss Holroyd felt that time, not instruction, would correct it. One day she would simply see it as it was, and that would be that.

Life at Briarcliffe suited Blanche so well that she was reluctant to go home for Christmas, until Sharon mentioned Cora. Cora had given up writing to people, at least to Sharon, but she welcomed letters from Blanche. Sharon sent her a brief Christmas greeting but received no reply. On her return Blanche explained that a blizzard had kept them in Madge's house and Ned's new basement, where she played Parcheesi with her father and with the Ouija board with Caroline. Madge and Caroline had had colds. Fayrene and Avery had come over with a new baby, on New Year's.

The cold she brought back from Norfork she gave to Sharon, chronically subject to bronchial infections. She was helpful to Sharon, the weekend she spent in bed, but found the time to compose a letter to her father. Sharon observed her: a tranquil study someone like Vermeer might have painted. Her head rested on her left arm, as if she were napping, while she scrawled the oval letters on a pad of paper. She was being a dutiful child, no more, but it piqued Sharon, lying there with her sniffles and cough while she wrote it. She sealed and went off with it without asking Sharon for a stamp.

The express ride on the North Side elevated brought her to Sharon on weekends, and the Lincoln Park Zoo, as the weather altered, was there just a short walk to the east. At the school she wore the green uniform of her classmates, with the bib at her front and the romperlike bloomers, but Sharon had been careful to outfit her in clothes that emphasized her adolescence. Knee-length stockings somewhat filled out her legs, and firmly attached her to low-heeled patent-leather oxfords, with straps. Her blue straw floater, with a pale yellow ribbon, held in place by an elastic chin strap, she wore tilted back on her head. Two long braids of hair hung free of her back as she walked, dangling ribbons to her waist. Not a girl, it seemed to Sharon, an idling male would molest. She always carried a sketch pad, a red pencil box, a blue purse she held by its strap, and often a paper bag with bread scraps for the pigeons and squirrels. It distressed Sharon to know that she also ate them herself, nibbling on them like cheese.

On weekends Blanche might receive several phone calls from Libby Pollitt, one of the day students, who lived at home in Evanston. Libby shared one of Blanche's afternoon botany classes, and was an avid specimen collector. She called Blanche to tell her of the strange things she had found. "Might I speak to Miss Kibbee?" she would ask Sharon, usually breath-

154

ing hard from the climb to her room. Blanche would sit cross-legged on the floor, beside the telephone stand, picking at bits of nap on the hallway rug. Libby's monologue might go on for as long as forty minutes, with no audible comment from Blanche. Sharon had spoken with Libby's mother, Gladys Pollitt, who had called to apologize for her daughter. Her other children were boys, and she found them quite a relief. On Mondays Libby would share with Blanche the specimens she had found on the weekend, which Blanche would bring home in a shoe box and store away in jelly jars with holes poked in the lids.

Sharon felt it would be a special pleasure to Blanche to have a friend of her own, who loved to talk to her, but after each of these calls she was noncommittal. Perhaps her apparent indifference was deceptive, since not once, to Sharon's knowledge, did she forget to tend the seeds and creatures stored away in jars on her window sill. Sharon herself marveled to see the caterpillar become a butterfly, which Libby would then add to her butterfly collection. Nor did chloroforming the creature and piercing it with a pin disturb Blanche as it did Sharon. Blanche was free to grow anything she might care to, but Sharon drew the line about the pin piercing. Discussing this with Blanche, Sharon had been painfully aware of not closing the gap she sensed between them. The child listened, wetting the tip of her finger to pick up crumbs from the table, which she had learned from Cora.

Sharon regretted the commute on the north shore elevated until she found that Blanche was so thrilled by it she often rode it farther than necessary and had to ride back. The big express train went too fast for Sharon, so high above the streets, with no visible support, but Blanche seemed captivated by both trains and streetcars. On the Clark Street car, when they rode into the Loop, she had to go stand at the front of the car, directly behind the motorman. She liked the clang of the bell, the way the car seemed to rock and dip on the tracks. It was so easy for Sharon to keep an eye on Blanche, her head rising above those around her, that Sharon did not feel the customary apprehension of parents with teen-aged children. On Saturday or Sunday they might attend the matinee at the movie house on Sheridan Avenue. Of course, Blanche had gone to movies with her father, in Norfork, but her avidity for them, the way her eyes "drank them in" (no other words so well described her rapt, wide-eyed enchantment), both amused and disturbed Sharon. Where was she off to, at such moments? In the darkness of the theater, as in a séance, she was exposed and vulnerable in a way that Sharon had never experienced. Yet when she stepped from the lobby into the glare of the street, what she had seen passed from her like a shadow. She saw only movies acceptable to Sharon, so it was hard to judge what types she preferred. The flickering light from the screen revealed her rapt attention, the skin about her mouth glistening with the butter and salt of her popcorn. Eating was part of her absorption. Her sister Caroline drove Madge almost dotty recounting the details of her latest movie, but Blanche soaked them in in a manner that left no trace. If Sharon troubled to ask her, she might nod that she had liked what she had seen.

Returning from her spring vacation in Norfork, her nose sunburned from the day she had spent with Cora, Blanche brought with her the sheet music of "Lotus Land," which Caroline had played for her on Cora's player piano. Sharon thought it pretentious, sentimental music of the worst kind. Blanche simply adored it. Would Sharon play it for her? Would Sharon teach her to play it? Sharon did play it for her, attentive, during the pauses, to the way Blanche sat on the bench at her side, drinking it in through her eyes and parted lips.

Fortunately, for them both, she was soon back at the school and had other interests by the following weekend. But Sharon had been shaken. Was it possible that Blanche would come, in her own slow time, to everything that Sharon had assumed and hoped she had put behind her? The ease she had felt in her presence gradually diminished. Her habitual silences, once so comforting, now weighed on her. What *was* on her mind? Twice monthly, now, Blanche wrote to her father, who addressed his letters to her to the school. That piqued Sharon. What was he concealing from her? On her February birthday, to Sharon's embarrassment, he sent her a large box of stale drugstore candy.

From her home in Charlottesville, Shirley Caudwell wrote to Blanche, enclosing a snapshot of herself on horseback. She wanted Blanche to come and visit her in the summer. Would she like to? Although Blanche liked horses, she was silently noncommittal. Sharon felt obliged to point out that if she visited Shirley she would meet her three sisters, see their wonderful farm, and be driven about in a tassel-fringed buggy. Blanche's habit, while listening to Sharon, was to crumble up pieces of her art-gum eraser and shoot them across the table with a flick of her fingernail. More vexing to Sharon was her habit of trying to conceal the very food she was eating, as if it were something stolen, or denied her, slipping it into her mouth with her head to one side, covertly. Was that something she had learned at the school? Sharon was reluctant to bring it up since it would surely diminish her interest in food. It would be just like her to simply stop eating, rather than be observed.

Late in April, a warm drizzly Saturday, the trees leafing, Sharon walked through the park to the pond boathouse, where she was accustomed to meet Blanche for a soft drink or a dish of ice cream. Because of the drizzle, only water birds were out on the pond. Blanche was usually at a table she liked in the café, from where she could look out over the lagoon, but she was neither there nor down on the pier where the boats were rented. A long-suppressed anxiety regarding Blanche surged up in her like a fever. She waited ten minutes, then went back along the walk that led to the birdhouse. The only person she passed was an elderly man with a dog. Just to the right of the walk, in a storage shed where food was kept for the animals, her eye was caught by bales of yellow hay, almost luminous in the dim light. Seated on one of the bales, huddled closely, so that both could stroke a bird in the girl's lap, a young man in overalls and red rubber boots had his left arm about the girl's waist. Her head was lowered to look at the bird that she held, her legs dangling just short of the straw-littered floor. With one hand she held the bird, some sort of exotic chicken, and with the other she stroked its plumed, brightly hued topknot. The young man's arm tightened about her waist as he inclined his head to touch her hair. Not lost on Sharon was his silly, conspiratorial smile. The sound that escaped her, an intake of breath, led the young man to glance up. Sharon stared at his beardless, oafish face, then he was gone into the barn's shadows. Hardly aware of what had happened, Blanche raised her head to look at Sharon.

"Oh, Aunt Sharon! Look at the bird."

With an effort, Sharon moved to look at it closely. Under its topknot was the head of a chicken.

"Where did you get it?"

"He brought it to me—" She looked behind her, then back to Sharon.

"We'd better see it's put back where it belongs," said Sharon, but Blanche would not be rushed. She stroked the bird, its eyes hypnotically half-lidded. Did Sharon feel they were much alike?

"Did you forget," Sharon said, "that you were going to meet me?"

Yes, it seemed she had forgotten. "He brought me the bird."

"You know him?"

"Oh, yes. His name is Jerry. He's nice."

As Sharon waited, she slipped off the bale of hay, permitted Sharon to dust off her skirt. They walked together in the drizzle to a caretaker raking up manure in one of the outdoor cages. "We found this bird," Sharon said. "Would you take him?"

Blanche was reluctant to release it.

"It has its own friends," Sharon said.

"Not that one," replied the man. "That one's a troublemaker." He took the bird from her, leaned his rake on the fence, and went off with it.

"Chickens are birds," said Blanche. "Did you know that?"

Actually, Sharon had not known it. Like Cora, she would have said that a chicken was a chicken. They walked together back to the apartment, where Sharon made some cinnamon toast. Nothing more was said of the matter. How close, Sharon wondered, had she come to an incident from which she, if not Blanche, might never have recovered? During the evening Blanche drew pictures of the bird's head with its half-lidded eyes.

Sunday evening, with Blanche returned to the school, Sharon called Madge to say that Blanche's year of schooling was drawing to a close. She had had a wonderful year, she was poised with people, could assert herself, and had put on some weight that showed in her face. But Sharon was now clear in her mind that what Blanche wanted most was her daddy and the closeness of her family. She was not a city girl. Madge was relieved to hear her say so, because her father had been wondering why they had her in the first place if she wasn't at home where they could enjoy her, before she got married.

The days and nights Cora was unable to leave the house the world shrank to accommodate her. The farm was what she could see through the porch screen, or the curtains at the front window, the air rising in a shimmer of heat from the graveled road. In the cooling dusk her vision blurred at the pump shed, as if the wick of the lamp had been lowered. From a clump of foliage low on the trunk, dead barkless branches forked from a tree Emerson had planted. The tree was cutting back, as they were.

Although she was first up, Cora waited for Emerson

to clear away the cobwebs blocking the door of the outbilly. When he sat down to breakfast they dangled like bits of veil from the rim of his straw hat. He smoked less, no longer able to keep the tobacco in the bowl of his pipe burning, nor did he complain, as he once did, of the weight at the pit of his stomach.

In October Emerson went with Avery to a cattle sale in O'Neill. It had been Cora's impression Emerson had gone to buy a cow, but he returned with a team of plow horses, it being the noise of tractors, in Avery's opinion, that cut down on the cows' milk. So the two horses would work better as a team, Avery gelded the white stallion.

Several days later Cora heard a loud whacking noise near the barn. From the porch she saw Avery tugging at the bridle of the stationary white horse. Emerson stood at the rear, holding a board from the fence, which he whacked across the horse's broad rump. The horse stood straddle-legged, as if watering, and looked swollen to Cora in his rear quarters. Neither the tugging on the bridle nor the whacking provoked him to move. Aloud Cora called, "What are you men up to?"

"He won't eat," Avery replied. "We got to exercise him."

Emerson let up whacking the beast to stroke the flank where the harness had worn away the white hair. "Lookee here," he said to the horse. "You ain't even a white horse, you're black." He patted the rump he had just been whacking, chuckling to himself. This commingling of affection and cruelty bewildered

Cora. An injury long forgotten, buried deep in her nature, reappeared as stabs of pain in the knuckles of her right hand. Emerson continued to whack the horse with the board while Avery tugged at the bridle. Flies rose in a cloud from his rump with each whack. Cora remained on the porch until both men had tired and left the creature to the swarm of flies, too weak to swish his tail. They retired to the shade of the pump house, where they drank buttermilk and discussed the problem. She could see Emerson when he thrust his head forward to spit. Her mind blank, a babble of voices filled Cora's ears. She had been here on the porch in a pause in her ironing, and Sharon's voice had carried as if spoken from a pulpit. Cora had been speechless, but Madge had said, "Mama, she don't mean it the way you hear it." It might have been last summer, it might have been this morning, Cora standing in the pickle-sharp draft off the kitchen, except that now she knew, as she hadn't before, that Sharon Rose had meant it just as she had said it. It had not been a horse that bit her; she had bitten herself.

Such things concerned her but did not distress her. If Sharon Rose were to ask her, she would now tell her. Cora had not felt then, nor did she feel now, that she might have led a different life—only that this life might have been led differently. Things she had once put from her mind now returned for her to ponder. How could one avoid hearing, or saying, more than what one said?

The hedge on the east, the light glare to the south, the heat to the west, bounded her domain. The air within the house was like that in the cobhouse, now used by the hens to roost in. The clapboards on the west side of the house were like dead bark-peeled branches. Emerson had once painted as high as he could reach, but he couldn't stand heights. He was now too old to do it from a ladder. He would say, "Come to think of it . . ." then forget what he thought. Otherwise he had mostly changed for the better. Rosalene and Blanche adored him. Cora might find him in the cobhouse, husking popcorn, or in the barn mending harness he no longer had use for. Over the winter he sat in her kitchen with his shoes off, his feet in the oven, comparing Montgomery Ward's with Sears Roebuck's prices. In the drought they needed water. They would drill a deeper well and pump it up. Ned would run pipes to Cora's parched garden, where the sweet corn shriveled before it flowered. Buckets of the water she carried disappeared into the caked earth. According to Emerson, the drought was due to a cloudburst they had had in '28. In the space of three hours the buckets left near the barn had filled with water and overflowed. The whole yard had looked like a lake. All that water had to come from somewhere, and it had come down in a single downpour. In his own mind he doubted it would ever rain again. The fault lay with a government that tinkered with farming, and ended wrecking the rain machinery. If in a long life he was sure of anything, he was sure of that.

When Ned and Madge had married, Cora's garden had grown more than they could eat, or had the need to put up. Fruit ripened and rotted with no need to pick it. There was so much to eat Cora had simply forgotten the year they lived out of cans. Then it rained less, and blew more, with the only moisture where the snow melted. Along with the dryness the spells of heat might last several weeks, without cooling nights. A drying wind rattled the wind wheel, pumping just enough water for the two cows.

Once green as a park, with dew on it in the morning, Cora's yard was the color of dried hay. The snow-flattened weeds near the barns were too matted to mow. In the evening fireflies rose from the fields of yellow grain like sparks. Buried in the yard somewhere were the croquet wickets, which always tripped Avery and his children. Only Cora seemed to see the mounds where the lost balls were buried. She meant to dig them up when it was warmer, but the stooping made her dizzy. If Madge brought the girls out to the farm they played cards for keeps on the screened-in porch. If the cards were taken away from Caroline she would play marbles for keeps with boys. She loved to win. If she couldn't win, she would cheat. She would rather lose than just play for the fun of it.

Caroline was a pudgy, brown-skinned girl who made people think of Shirley Temple. In Cora's opinion, the child was a show-off. A willful streak in her nature would lead her to do just the opposite of what was expected. Just as Madge had once sat and ogled Sharon, Blanche would sit and ogle Caroline. The seed of independence, the school principal had told

Madge, was often dormant in some natures until it suddenly sprouted. In most other respects Blanche was the image of Cora, already taller than her mother and thin as a rake.

Was it that summer or the next one that the two men came out from the government, in Lincoln, to give advice to Emerson. They found him in the barn seated on the treadwheel, sharpening a scythe. Cora could hear its sharp rasp above their talk, as he let them wait. What did they want? They wanted to help him. They followed him to the house with their coats folded over their arms. They seemed friendly enough to Cora, asking her about her chickens, and her children. The older one had a son in the college at Lincoln. From the upstairs window opening out on the porch roof Emerson called to them to leave his farm. They replied that they had only come out to help him. Through the screen of the upper window Emerson fired his shotgun into the tree that shaded the porch. The men ran to where they had left their car, then drove through the hedge to get to the driveway. Cora felt that Emerson had acted too strongly, but she understood his feelings. It could never be so bad that accepting charity wouldn't make it worse.

To Cora's amazement, Madge found a spoon buried in the grounds in her coffeepot. She could not understand it. The coffee had tasted the same. It angered her to watch Madge make a wad of her dishtowel to wipe the bottoms of Cora's clean cups. Why in the world did she? It proved to be dust, fine as talcum, visible when she drew a line on the oilcloth, or moved a plate. This dust puffed in a cloud when Cora shook out a curtain, or fussed with the doilies on a dresser. Emerson's socked feet swept a shiny path between the bed and the hallway. Cora had not observed it until Fayrene pointed it out. Her own attention had been focused on the room off the kitchen, where the pattern had been worn off the linoleum. It proved to be too intricate to replace, but Cora brightened up the area with daubs of green and white paint. She went from there, having the paint, to daub white on the steps in the stairwell so they were visible in the dark. The iron frame of the bed, painted white, glowed in the dark like a presence. With the last brushful of the paint she touched up the hardware on the doors and the rusted metal handles of the stovepipe dampers. Emerson made no comment, knowing his way about without the need to look.

It seemed to Cora that he walked about in his sleep. She might see him in the yard, his big hands dangling, standing in the shadow cast by his hat, or moving slowly between the house and the barn with his head tilted forward, the sun on his neck. He had grown so spare his thighs no longer rubbed. It startled him when Cora, in her high shrill voice, called him to supper. He ate with his hat on, there no longer being a reason to take it off. Cats no longer followed him to the house after the milking, there being too little in the pail to slosh. Cora now let it set and skimmed off the cream, to spare herself the work of cleaning the separator. Avery brought them butter and cheese curds from the creamery. She had her chores. She never seemed to lack for something to do.

She heard the bang of Emerson's hammer on one of the porch posts, but she did not hear him fall. Fearing ladders, he had climbed on a chair to mend a hole in the screen. His straw hat had fallen off, and he sat on the ground, wagging his head. With her help he got to his feet, but it made him dizzy to stand. He lay down on the cot and Cora sat with him, fanning off the flies. He made no complaint. Perhaps the swish of the fanning lulled him to nap. A gray beard darkened his sunken jowls; his lips were compressed to hold his chew in. Cora had had few occasions to study his face. The corners of his mouth and the tips of his mustache were the color of tobacco. Above the ridge left by his hat his forehead was dough-colored, without wrinkles. The fanning of the air stirred the wisps of hair about his ears. They looked huge to Cora, like the shells used to prop open doors. It shamed her to look at him with his eyes closed, feeling in her soul he was a stranger to her, and she to him. He had struck one of his fingers with the hammer and the blood oozed black around the blue nail. He seemed indifferent to the flies crawling on his hands.

This impression of Emerson would displace all others in Cora's mind. He had never appeared young to her. It had been his easy assurance that impressed her. All of that now seemed part of a tranquil past unrelated to this present. The trip from Ohio, Emerson seated beside her, or going before her, walking the horses, now seemed a journey in the other direction. She was lulled by the creak of the harness; Emerson seemed short-legged in the tall grass. Over and over she saw him open his coin purse and spill the coins into the palm of his hand. Sorting the nails from the coins seemed to please him. Over and over she saw him wind his watch without checking the time. About this journey she had had no foreboding that it would conclude with a nightmare. Emerson still went before her, but they seemed to journey backward, into the past.

In Dr. Schirmer's opinion, Emerson had suffered a stroke. This had caused him to fall from the chair and experience dizzy spells when Cora helped him. Over Cora's objections, a Battle Creek woman stayed in the house for a week, bringing her knitting with her, and a radio. Cora slept in the bedroom upstairs, where she could hear the music through the floor ventilator. It seemed inexcusable she would play her radio while being paid to nurse. Cora walked about the house, her arms crossed at her front, or sat in the rocker on the screened-in porch, her fingers touching her lips, her right elbow cupped in her left palm. If she peered in on Emerson, he looked peaceful.

The Battle Creek woman, Mrs. Berger, had lost her husband in the first war and her eldest son, Lincoln, in the second. Her daughter was married and living in Sioux City. She would rather be a visiting nurse than sit alone at home. Cora was not drawn to her, but stewed a chicken which she served with succotash and pickle relish. Without her radio the house seemed silent. At night Cora would wander about with the smoking lamp, as if looking for something that was missing. The stale air of the house smelled of the mothballs found in the pockets of Emerson's dress suit. After forty years of wear the knees bulged, but the coat looked new.

Like Orion, Emerson lived through the winter until it was March and the snow melted. He was so peaceful, Cora needed the assurance of Ned and Madge that he was dead. Blanche ran off and hid where neither Rosalene nor Caroline could find her. "Let her be," said Madge. "She's looking for him." Emerson had never liked the Battle Creek pastor, but that was where both Orion and Belle were buried. Where the earth appeared to be sunken a space was reserved for Cora. In the shade of the trees the women sat in the cars, fanning the air with newspapers. The light glared; a chill wind blew into Cora's face. But Madge remarked that Emerson would like it now that the trees were grown. There were neighbors at the service whose names Cora had forgotten, or never known. How strange the men looked to be standing in the open without their hats. They wore the solemnly blank expressions of young heifers lined up at a fence. She thought of Sharon, but she put from her mind what had been said.

For Cora to live on the farm alone was unthinkable, until they thought it. It was what she knew. Who else would know where to look for the eggs? As soon as he could, with the war ended, Ned would put in her inside toilet. She would burn cobs in the range to cook, but oil in the coal burner for heat. In January she could visit with Madge if the feuding of the girls didn't drive her crazy, which it did. Madge called her twice a week to chat, and ask how she was. When Cora said that at her age one day was like another, but the nights were different, she felt shooting pains where the horse had bit her, that's what she had felt. Only later, when she thought about it, did it occur to her that it had not been a horse.

The old tree that had once shaded the house now let in so much light she had to keep the shades drawn. Everywhere she went, in the barn or the pump shed, in the cobhouse or the storm cave, or where the rakes and harrows were overgrown with grass, or along the cow trail that led to the pasture, she would find something Emerson had put down and forgotten to pick up. A tool or a hoe, pieces of grindstone, the blade of a scythe without the handle, the right hand of a pair of gloves, taken off so he could search his pockets for matches. In the muck of the stable, a pair of rubber boots. In the pocket of a sweater on a nail in the barn, a lump of half-sucked hoarhound in a piece of bread wrapper. She left it in the pocket, but brought the sweater back to a hook on the porch.

Boards in the sheds broke under her weight, little as it was. In the upstairs bedrooms bats whooshed through the holes in the screens, stirring the curtains. In the seat of the platform rocker she found an egg. Were the hens moving in with her? It confounded her to ponder how it had got there. In a dresser drawer full of Fayrene's doll clothes she found what had once been kittens. By lamplight she darned the stockings Madge brought her, the screen at her back crawling with insects. In the winter she did afghans and quilts.

Madge and Ned came upon her seated on the bed holding the bean bag dolls she had made from flour sacks. Madge had called and called but Cora had not answered the phone. Cora was given her choice: she could share a room with Blanche, in Madge's house, or she could go live with Fayrene, in her new house. The week she spent with Blanche, Ned, and Madge, Cora did not eat. They had had the same problem when they visited the fair, and nothing had worked until they took her home. Fayrene found it easier, far as it was, to drive from O'Neill to the farm, two or three times a week, and look in on her. The door to the upstairs was bolted so she wouldn't fall when she walked about at night. She told Madge that Belle had come over to visit her. From the room off the kitchen she had spoken to Cora, never showing her face. "Is that you, Belle?" she had asked, but there was no mistaking it had been Belle's voice. Often the drone of thronging bees filled her ears like water. Fayrene didn't have the time to go and look for her if she wasn't in the house. She would clean up a bit, then put food out on the table, which she hoped Cora would get before the mice did. Fayrene told Madge when she first had the feeling that the person eating the food wasn't Cora. She couldn't prove it, of course. But that was how she felt. She took Ardene, her grandchild, along with her when she paid a visit to the farm. The child had turned in the yard to look back and see Cora standing in the door of the barn, holding a syrup pail. Ardene had simply not been able to speak. Cora had turned away, and later Fayrene and Avery had found the syrup pail in the cobhouse, full of eggs. Before winter they would have to do something. They agreed to that.

Against the morning chill Cora might be seen in Orion's stocking cap, pulled down over her ears, one of Emerson's old sweaters with holes in the pockets. If strangers happened to see her, she would greet them like friends, saying, "Come in where it's cool," and open the screen. Madge and Fayrene took turns stopping by the farm. One day they found the fire in the range had died, the water boiled out of the kettle. Madge went to look for her at Orion's place, but it was Rosalene who found her crouched on a milk stool in the cobhouse, unable to get up. Tightly gripped in one hand she held the cob she had been using to hand-shell popcorn, the white kernels loose in the pouch of her apron. Her eyes were wide, but Madge could not get her to speak. What had she wanted with popcorn, without her teeth?

Some would say that Madge, against Cora's will, should have taken her into her home in Norfork. A person so old is not able to best judge her own good. They agreed, however, that it was her chores that kept her going as long as she did. Hearing voices she would say, "Come in where it's cool," as if the lawn before her was green as winter wheat, the sky blue as ice, the light clear as rain water. Chores would come to her without her need to know what they were.

Between President Kennedy's assassination and her first stroke, there was nothing so unusual in the family that Madge had to call Sharon to tell her about it. One thing followed another. Madge sometimes wondered if anyone in the family would notice if it didn't.

Ned Kibbee's always doing as he pleased, which meant building no more houses than he cared to, soon found him employed as a carpenter to a builder of tract houses in Lincoln. This man built nice, up-to-date houses for almost a third less than Ned could build them. He paid Ned a good wage but the work he did gave him little satisfaction. The younger men were gone before he got to know them, or they sat around during the lunch break talking about girls and football. Ned had never played games. That they were now played by grown men who did nothing else left him bewildered. He shared this perplexity with the elderly widow who operated the motel where he spent his week nights. She confessed to him, with embarrassment, that she spent hours of each day watching the TV in the office. It was there for the guests, but during the periods of idleness it helped her pass the time. The people she saw in the serials were the only people she saw often enough to feel that she knew them. When one of them died she felt it as a personal loss. Mrs. Mullen had been living in Lincoln when the Starkweather boy, and the girl he had, committed all those senseless murders, so it had not come as such a surprise to her when the President was assassinated. She no longer felt she really understood young people, including five of her own. Ned Kibbee had never felt that other people's business was in any way whatsoever his own business, but evenings he spent with Mrs. Mullen led him to reflect more on what he saw around him, little of which he liked.

Madge had been slowed up for several years before she had her stroke. The stroke simply brought it to people's attention, and in some ways that made it easier for her. Fayrene Dickel, or one of her girls, would stop and do what Blanche couldn't do for her. She sat more. There was not a lot for her left to do but eat. Fayrene would have given her a TV but Madge really liked what she heard better than what she saw. It was hard for her to ignore what she didn't like if she was watching it. All the years that they had had Blanche around the house, and all the things Blanche had learned without Madge's troubling to tell her, proved to be so helpful Madge often wondered if that was not the way it had been intended. Blanche had always been happy in the things she did for others, and with more to do she was happier than ever.

If Madge got worse, which was more likely than her ever getting better, Blanche would be able to take care of Ned even better than Madge had. She loved her daddy, but Madge admitted there was truth in Caroline's saying that Ned often treated her like a pet.

Blanche was not to be likened to anything but herself, her contentment in doing what she happened to be doing, her willingness to do whatever Madge suggested, her delight in anything that was done for her, and her unchanging, unspoken, unreasonable aversion to Caroline. When they were little girls Madge had thought they might be like herself and Sharon Rose, drawn together by their differences, but Caroline, a little magpie as a child, could never accept Blanche's silence. Together they were like pickles and ice cream. Caroline was like Sharon in her early resentment that she should like boys more than she did girls, but she was not at all like Sharon in the impression she made on people. She was like her father, but in a man it didn't rile people up so much.

No one could look at Fayrene Dickel and imagine what she had been like as a girl. After five girls of her own she was still thin as a rail, with more to do socially than she could find the time for. Her complexion was rough, under the powder, but there was hardly a sign of the acne that once made it hard for Madge to look at her. Her eldest daughter, Eileen, had persuaded her to wear a two-tone wig. To recall what she had looked like as a girl Madge had to look at Maureen, who had her father's gray eyes but Fayrene's buck teeth before she lost them. Fayrene had found it hard to speak when she came to live with Madge, but now, as Ned said, just try to shut her up. Madge liked her. She was as full of life as a box of kittens. With Avery's success she had a big new home she could hire people to keep clean for her. On a camping trip to Yellowstone Park she took Blanche along as if she was one of her family. Privately, Madge felt that Fayrene looked better with her own gray hair and glasses without gems on them, but there were things Madge did, like doze off during meals, to which Fayrene took exception but didn't complain about.

Avery Dickel was a hulking, easygoing man, liked almost as much by people as he was by animals. He still had his bushy hair, white now at the temples, and there were people who thought he should run for public office. He was the first to hire a woman veterinarian to handle the small pets in his office. Dogs had always liked Avery, and would follow his car if they weren't chained up. Entirely on her own Caroline went directly to Avery when she needed the money for two years of graduate school. If money proved to be a problem all the girls knew that they could turn to Avery for it, and with that understanding most of the problems worked themselves out.

None of Fayrene's girls were particularly attractive but they all seemed to appeal to boys. The prettiest, Eileen, who looked like Avery's mother, was so thin they mistakenly thought she was frail. Yet who but Eileen would be the first of the girls to have a son. Madge had thought that Eileen would have to be more forward if she wanted to get the attention of boys, but her shy, almost bashful manner actually attracted some boys to her. She never lacked for attention, if that was what she wanted. If she had been Madge's child they might have seen more of Sharon Rose.

There was one thing that happened, but it was so unusual Madge preferred not to think about it. Caroline had given both counsel and money to a Lehigh girl who had an abortion. Madge's great fear had been that something might pop out of Caroline in her sleep.

Fayrene had got into genealogy through a Mormon boy who had been sweet on Eileen. Her main interest had been people with all-girl families. Both the Atkinses and the Averys went back to England, the Atkinses as far as the seventeenth century. Where they went before that was anybody's guess. Fayrene's youngest girl, Maureen, now in her second year at dental college, had flown to England with her friend Billie Gaines where they cycled alone all over Hampshire. Maureen admired Caroline, and Blanche could see in how many ways she would have her problems, especially with boys.

After the Second World War Sharon Rose settled down to teach in Wellesley, just a short ride from Boston. Her best friend was Monica Searles, who taught piano and voice, and accompanied Yvette Bonnel in her song recitals. Sharon thought Yvette's voice was both small and strained, but over the years Monica had grown accustomed to it. Being the only one who drove a car, and more practical by nature, Monica helped Sharon with her chores on those days she was not assisting Yvette. It had proved a mistake for the three of them to lunch or shop together. Monica reserved Sundays for Sharon, and they would drive to a country inn for dinner, then return to Boston for the symphony program. Monica was partial to Charles Munch, but Sharon thought he lacked Koussevitzky's feeling. Neither Monica nor Sharon cared to fly, but they had twice gone by steamer to England, and from there to the musical season in Zurich. Monica was hardly taller than Sharon, nervous in manner, and given to food allergies and fretting, but loyal and affectionate by nature. She looked after Yvette on Mondays, Wednesdays and Fridays, and the other four days she devoted to Sharon. It piqued Sharon to reflect that she told them both to rest and avoid drafts. Sharon took long daily walks on the Wellesley campus, which reminded her so much of parts of England, reserving the late morning for her piano students. Perhaps she was more respected by her students than liked. Young women "into music," especially the piano, were prone to almost feverish attachments to their teachers, which proved detrimental to their studies. Monica deplored this as much as Sharon, but she never seemed to learn from her experience. Each year she had several new close attachments, followed by painful withdrawals. All these young women were ignorant of what it cost Sharon to spare them what she had not been spared herself. It was known to them all that she had once "given freely of herself" and been hurt.

Sharon did indulge herself in allowing Monica, four years her senior, her health hardly robust, to fuss over her and run errands at the expense of time and energy she might have devoted to the hopelessly dependent Yvette. Sharon allowed her dislike of Yvette to result in this self-indulgent, uncharitable behavior, feeling that if Monica insisted on caring for people, it might as well be her.

A last letter from Lillian Baumann, shortly after the war, began with affectionate memories of their meeting in Lincoln, their growing closeness in Chicago and London, then ended abruptly to avoid an expression of her increasing bitterness. War had shattered the

England she loved. Sharon had failed her expectations. After Lillian's death, her friend Ivy Moseley had returned to Sharon a packet of her letters to Lillian, which Ivy had left unread. Giving oneself to the past was even more fruitless than giving oneself to others. Sharon found life acceptable without the need to flatter or think well of herself.

Ln October the plain is dry as dust, but
through the windows of the airport it glistens as if
freshly painted. When the glass vibrates it appears to
quiver, as if alive. Football fans, wearing red hats and
red jackets, stream in and out the doors, crowd into
taxis. The two women who stand at the Travelers Aid
counter are old enough to evaluate their conflicting
impressions. One has come back to where she started
and took the greatest pains to get away from. Unless
sprinkled with regrets, she is thinking, happiness is a
shallow emotion. Nevertheless, she feels more at

home than she had been led to expect. She stands near, and appears to be part of, a large display of pumpkins, ears and stalks of corn, as well as bundles and vases of dried arrangements. These muted fall colors seem to have been chosen to harmonize with the outfit she is wearing. Her hat is forest green, with a pheasant's feather, the jacket of tan gabardine over a straw-colored blouse with a gold pin at the throat. Suede shoes with low heels match her hat. A coiled braid of silver hair is gathered to a bun at the nape of her neck. It has always been Sharon Rose's feeling, and her practice, that to be in good taste is to be inconspicuous.

Her companion, an exact foot taller, wears a black sleeveless cape over a habit (it is the word that comes to mind) of the color made famous by the order of Gray Mothers. She is hatless; her short, crisp hair is worn in a mannish pompadour. Few trouble to notice its color. Her beak-nosed face, the erect posture that seems to tilt her slightly backward, enhance the impression of a figure designed to symbolize something. There is nothing about her that is not conspicuous.

Just the moment before, the name of Sharon Rose Atkins had been hawked over the public address system. It made no visible impression on the throng that milled about as if lost. A young woman in a uniform designed by a man, which called attention to her squat unfortunate figure, came toward Sharon, leading three elderly people, one a male. Out of long habit the two women trailed behind him, a slow vehicle in fast traffic. The brim of his sweat-stained hat had been wiped back so that he could see better, but it didn't help. Confronting Sharon Rose, he blinked his eyes. He had expected something more substantial.

"You're Miss Atkins?"

Sharon nodded. To gain time he blew his nose, dabbed the cloth at his eyes. The tall stooped woman directly behind him gazed at Sharon as if she were a child in a manger. She said, "You've got a brother named Walter?"

"No."

"A sister Gloria?"

"No."

The old man stepped back to gain perspective. A topcoat was draped over his shoulders. His long gray face cocked to the left to put his better eye in focus.

"You're not Adelaide?" No, Sharon Rose was not Adelaide. She felt the keenness of the woman's disappointment. In a gesture that startled Sharon, and held her eyes, the woman put her fingers to her lips as if to hush them. The man turned to face the women. "She says it ain't her."

"Well, I suppose she knows."

"There must be other Atkins," said Sharon.

"Not with Walter for a brother," the woman replied. She seemed to feel this refuted Sharon's position.

"I don't think it's her," the other woman said. "She wouldn't be so small."

Hearing that, the man wheeled and led them off. The rear view of the tall stooped woman with the narrow shoulders, one hand clutching her purse, one held out from her side as if gripping an invisible pail, held Sharon's attention. Her feet, in unaccustomed shoes, were not at home on the lobby's smooth surface.

For the second time on the same day, Sharon had been mistaken for somebody else. *I'm Sharon Atkins,* she had said. Didn't she look it? She felt the need to check on her appearance. Someone who knew her— back here where she had come from—should step forward and reassure her. In the airport in Boston she had been approached by a woman both bizarre and distinguished in appearance, who now stood beside her. Tall, with short-cropped gray hair, wearing a cape over a smock. As if Sharon had beckoned to her, she said, "I'm Alexandra Selkirk," and put down her flight bag.

Sharon had returned her gaze.

"You're not Miss Gaylord?"

"I'm Sharon Atkins."

"Are you sure? You're not here to meet me?" She wheeled slowly to look about her. "I'm so seldom mistaken. Would it be Hayden something, instead of Gaylord?" She stooped to grope in her flight bag. "You're not Mrs. Chalmers? No, no, that's in Lincoln. I'm so sorry. Will you forgive me? I just can't believe that I'm mistaken." It was clear from her gaze that she did not believe it. A long lantern-jawed visage, unmistakably British, but no sign of it in her brusque speech. A person of impulses. What would she think of next?

"You mentioned Lincoln," said Sharon.

"Yes, yes. Lincoln, Nebraska." To assure herself, she referred again to a letter.

"Why," said Sharon, "that's where I'm going."

"You see!" she cried. "I knew it! We came here to meet each other!" Her mouth widened to reveal the gap where a tooth was missing. The others were widely spaced, tusk-like. Had she so little interest in her appearance? On Sharon's right shoulder she had rested her large left hand, gripped it firmly. Sharon's impulse to withdraw, to disengage, her most habitual and salient characteristic, seemed to be neutralized by the current of emotion that flowed between them. Long ago, on a similar occasion, she had asserted her independence. "Your fear of being beholden," Lillian had written, "is really just a fear of your own emotions." Never mind now what her emotions had been; had her fears been real? They no longer aroused the same emotions.

"Come!" Miss Selkirk said, and led her by the arm toward the gate to their plane.

Experienced with travel, experienced with people, she arranged that Sharon should sit beside her, on the aisle. "I've got to nap," she said. "I left London at midnight. My biorhythms are in confusion." She had a lecture to give—she paused to search in her bag for the room reservation—in Grand Island that evening. Where was Grand Island? Sharon explained. Alexandra asked the stewardess to tilt back her seat, then slipped about her head a pair of black eyeshades, held in place by a piece of elastic. Her face, with the eyes covered, was that of a corpse. Had she no idea how she looked? Sharon could not have exposed herself in this manner. A pleated upper lip, the pores of her nose like those of ripening berries, furrows everywhere, a curious absence of wrinkles, flesh as loose as gloves on her large-knuckled brown-splotched hands. Beneath the left jawbone, a slight swelling and discoloration, characteristic of violin players. Sharon might have guessed it. A woman of such emotion would have nourished herself through music. What music? She thought it might be Vivaldi, the strings urgent and vibrant, the rhythms coming at you like a change in the weather. Sharon would have liked to cover the large idle hands. They were scarless, but insinuating. A similar pair of hands had gripped her in such a manner that she could still feel them. Alexandra Selkirk napped, as if drugged, until they landed in Chicago, where two cups of black coffee revived her. From her purse she took a tin of mints, which she shared with Sharon, and a letter addressed to her in London confirming her reservation at the Crossways Inn. Crossways. How right that was! Women from all over the world would be there. Against her better judgment—and little it mattered—she had been persuaded to fly from England and keep the midwestern momentum going. That had been their appeal. Their *momentum!* Her laughter set her to choking; the stewardess brought her a glass of water.

She confessed to Sharon that she gave freely to strangers what she hesitated to admit to herself. Man's culture was a hoax. Was there a woman who didn't *feel* it? Perhaps a decade, no more, was available to women to save themselves, as well as the planet. Women's previous triumphs had been by default. Men had simply walked away from the scene of the struggle, leaving them with the children, the chores, the culture, and a high incidence of madness. In a brief résumé of her forthcoming lecture, Alexandra touched on the high points of woman's bondage and her emerging liberation. What saddened her was that she didn't believe it: not a word of it.

She was the daughter of an Army officer and mining engineer exiled in Casper, Wyoming. Her mother had died at her birth. Guilt, surely, had led her father to try to recover that loss in Alexandra. At nine pampered years of age she had been sent to school in the east. Still hardly more than a child, at a school in Geneva, she had married the son of a wine merchant and gone to his home in Grenoble. A darling boy, really, but his home had been her first internment camp. Nevertheless, she liked him as a person. It was the custom of the tribe that had made him a jailer. It had taught her that if you could change the customs, you could change the world. Just recently the flower children had done it, with results she found nauseating. But it *had* been done. More change in ten years than in the previous five centuries. Was it a flaw in her argument to find that customs indeed might change, but not women? A cat was a cat, a dog was a dog, but who could say what it was to be a woman? Without an image of who they were, *who* were they? Hadn't Sharon noticed? Many were seized with the mania to be many people. A curious fact. God knows where it might lead. Alexandra's discourse was punctuated by gasping inhalations of cigarette smoke. Her mouth open wide, her eyes lidded, the cloud of smoke would be visible in her throat the instant before inhalation. It seemed to Sharon little that went in found its way out.

Never before had Sharon felt drawn to such an aggressive, possessive person. One of her talon-like hands gripped her by the wrist, holding her like prey. A coincidence, surely, but Sharon was reminded of the confrontation with Cora, who had gripped her by the wrist as she whacked her with the hairbrush. Before their arrival in Lincoln, Alexandra took sodium pills to avoid possible heat prostration. She dropped silent as suddenly as she had begun to talk.

A portly matron, wearing owl-eyed tinted glasses, a driving cap with a duckbill visor, had recognized Alexandra from her pictures and identified herself as Mrs. Lura Chalmers, her host and chauffeur. Was there somewhere she could drop Sharon? Mrs. Chalmers's white face had no visible eyebrows; her smile was that of a performing minstrel. Sharon explained that she was waiting for one of her nieces. Why couldn't her niece, Alexandra asked, return Sharon to the Crossways Inn, in Grand Island, from where they could return to Boston together? Sharon didn't know. She heard Mrs. Chalmers offer to reserve her a room and look forward to the pleasure of her company on the drive back to Lincoln. Sharon preferred to be alone and collect her jumbled thoughts. She watched Alexandra, as did many others, cross the lobby with her cape billowing behind her, the portly matron trailing with her flight bag. Alexandra would prefer to take the wrong way, on her own, than be led in the right one. Moments passed before Sharon was aware of the woman at her side, staring at her. The way her right hand gripped the left arm, above the elbow, caught Sharon's attention before her face. She wore plaid-patterned loose-fitting shorts, freshly creased across the lap.

"You're Sharon Atkins?"

"I am," Sharon replied. Behind the large square-framed glasses, the round face seemed familiar. Sharon had previously remarked that feminist-type women were often of an indeterminate age. There were pencils and cards in the pocket of her blouse. The largeness of the glasses enhanced the smallness of her eyes.

"I'm Caroline Kibbee," she said.

Sharon blurted, "You are?" She had anticipated Sharon's surprise. She released her grip on the left arm to place both arms across her front. Sharon thought it a very unattractive posture. Caroline had been a brash button-eyed tomboy, the pride of her father, the despair of her mother. Insofar as possible Sharon had ignored her. She now had her mother's figure, her heavy thighs, but her father's dark hair and complexion. When she stooped to pick up Sharon's flight bag, the backside was unmistakably familiar. Dark hairs were visible on her bare legs.

"It's been so long!" Sharon prattled, but Caroline did not reply until they approached the exit, and she had it calculated.

"Thirty-three years," she said.

Sharon thought that impossible. She had been back, briefly, during the war, following Madge's first severe illness. Perhaps Caroline had not been there. She would have to think. Still, she might have said something further if the blast of heat at the entrance had not caught her breath. A shimmer of heat and light outlined Caroline's figure, the lumpy shadow that moved beside her. She turned to glance at Sharon, her lips compressed, then proceeded ahead of her across the parking area. Sharon lidded her eyes against the metallic glare. She almost thumped into Caroline, who said, "I left Carl and Crystal in the car. They came along for the ride." Sharon did not trouble to ask whose children they were. They walked with bowed heads to a car with a dented front fender, a child's face at one lowered rear window. Both children had perspiring faces, protruding teeth. "Let it air out," Caroline said, and cranked down the front windows. On the driver's side, a crumpled ironing pad covered a hole in the seat cushion. Curls of Blue Chip stamps were strewn across the dashboard. The short walk had left Sharon faintly dizzy. "Eileen don't like it much," Caroline said, "but Bryan says he can't buy both cars and tractors."

"Bryan?"

"He's their daddy," she replied, looking at the children. "They just come along for the ride."

"We come along for the ele-funt hall!" the girl hooted. Her unblinking button eyes seemed to challenge Sharon. The boy was less assured. Both wore T-shirts with faded football emblems.

The movement of air, as the car started, cooled the film of moisture on Sharon's face. "Lincoln's grown," said Caroline. "On football weekends it's got almost two hundred thousand people." Sharon registered disbelief. Through the grime-smeared windshield she could see little of the city. To miss the football traffic Caroline drove east, entering town on a street that skirted the fairgrounds. Sharon recognized nothing. Why were the elms so drab and rust-colored? "It's the blight," Caroline said. "All the elms have got it. If they can't do something, they're going to have to destroy them." Sharon would not have been able to say that. She would have said, "Something has to be done," and left it at that. "If there's no parking," Caroline went on, "I'm going to let you out and just drive around, then come back and pick you up. They want to see elephants, dinosaurs, or whatever."

The boy said, "I want to see the saber-toothed tiger."

"Their daddy tells them these stories," said Caroline, "but he won't take the time to bring them down here."

"They were here before we were," said Carl.

"Yes, and they'll be here when we're gone," replied Caroline. The edge in her voice surprised Sharon. What were the children to think? In the Hall of Elephants they would see monsters that would be here when they had vanished—not merely part of the past but most of the future. Wouldn't it give an imaginative child nightmares? Sharon thought briefly of Alexandra Selkirk: the pleasure she would feel in

Man's extinction—her sorrow at Woman's loss.

Just as Caroline had feared, there was no parking place, so Sharon was dropped off with the children in front of the elephant hall. Thanks to the football game, they had the exhibit to themselves. An elephant was there, remarkably lifelike, with long curving tusks, the trunk raised like a trumpet, but the huge creature was dwarfed by the world's largest mammal. An ancestor of the rhinoceros, this colossus was not from the plains around Lincoln, but from the vast wastes of Siberia. Whatever impression it left on the children, Sharon was transfixed. It had simply not been brought to her attention that the world contained such creatures. More than sixty feet long, twenty feet high, it was here among smaller monsters because no other hall was large enough for it. It was Sharon's impression that the beast bulked as large as the head seemed small. For millions of years, a mind-numbing abstraction, it had waddled about waiting for extinction. In due time it had come. This message—and it was a message—weighed upon Sharon like the heat. In displays along the walls were the skeletal remains of smaller creatures, one with tusks like the woolly mammoth. As a background the artist had depicted what might have been the appearance of the plains at that time, a fanciful landscape in pleasant somewhat muted fall colors, like those worn by Sharon. Here and there a strange beast might be seen wandering in a zoo of animal crackers. Also exhibits of bones, as the diggers had found them; exhibits of the tracks left by a vast reptile, the dinosaur. What had destroyed him? A change in the weather? Was he too well adapted to a marshy climate? Who could not see in this—it occurred to Sharon—the future of man in a world of women. This startling thought she owed to Alexandra Selkirk. A flight through time. Even at this moment the males were gathered in one of their primitive ceremonies, blind as the dinosaur to what was happening. It pleased Sharon to note that the girl, Crystal, showed the effects of an experience she would long remember, while her sniffling little brother wet his face at the water fountain. In the diggings of the future, the football coliseum would be the interment site of an extinct species. But why—she would ask Alexandra—had it taken so long?

A short visit proved to be long enough. Sharon bought them each a packet of arrowheads, and stamps, then they stood at the front waiting for Caroline. She had bought gasoline and had the windshield of the car cleaned. A few minutes later, north of the east-west freeway, Caroline turned in the seat to say, "Look back!"

The city of Lincoln, a shimmering mirage, rose from the rolling plain as Cora might have dreamed it. Dinosaurs had roamed here. The saber-toothed tiger had hunted the river canyons. At this moment a sampling of the state's population was watching a game of football. Sharon's mind was a jumble of confusing impressions. She let her head loll back on the seat. Now and then a lark's cry, distorted by the car's movement, fell on her ear as cool and liquid as water. In the back seat Crystal read aloud from the comic book spread on her lap. To keep her hair from blowing, Caroline had put on a straw hat, the elastic chin band puffing out her cheeks.

"How is Blanche?" Sharon asked. In Madge's letters she had always been "well," or "fine."

"You'll see her."

"She never married?"

"Aunt Sharon," Caroline said with emphasis, "we don't get married anymore unless we want to. We all had your example."

Her lips parted, Sharon let the wind dry her mouth. After a moment she said, "My *example?*"

"Was it boys you didn't like, or marriage?"

"I don't remember being asked."

"Mom said you could've married almost anybody."

Only Professor Grunlich came to Sharon's mind, along with a sigh of relief. "I wanted my independence," she said, "like you."

The answer appeared to satisfy Caroline. How much did these brash young women know? It startled her to think they might know more than she did. Caroline drove with one hand, her head tilted back, her free hand surfing on the air at the window. What was she thinking? That Sharon Rose had not feared to act, but feared to speak out? In the dark field they were passing, a huge piece of machinery, like a giant insect, sprayed the earth with revolving sprinklers, the spray blowing like smoke. A rainbow immaterial as a dragonfly's wing hovered between Sharon and the sky. The heat and shimmering light drugged her senses, weighed on her eyes. Unaware that her lips had parted, she heard the gourd-like sound of wind in her mouth. Dreamily disembodied, she eagerly held on to this fragile impression. Ned Kibbee was driving, the side curtains were flapping, Fayrene and Madge were talking, and in the fields rows of shocked corn basked in the diffused fall light. The wires dipped and rose, the poles and trees flicked past, and in the fabric of this fancy, like a patterned design, she sensed both something lost and something gained. Cora Atkins was dead. Madge had called her to say, "She went in her sleep. I hope I'm as lucky." Sharon did not believe in pain, but she had bridled when Madge had taken comfort from her death in sleep. After a long and humiliating illness, Lillian Baumann had died, her mind and soul wide awake.

"Aunt Sharon?" Caroline said.

"Yes."

"Did you ever see *Wanda?*"

Nobody of that name came to Sharon's mind. "Wanda who?"

"It's a movie."

"I see so few. Was it a good one?"

"It was horrible." At the thought of it, she grimaced. Her lips were set in a thin tight line.

"As bad as all that?"

"This woman. She's been married and had a baby. She's so beat and depressed she doesn't care about it, or anything else. She's so beat she's hardly human. A man picks her up. She's like a stray dog."

"Why did you go to see it?"

"It was on the TV."

"You couldn't turn it off?"

"No."

The finality of the no was disturbing. Sharon could not think of anything so appalling she wouldn't turn it off.

"That's where we're different," said Caroline. "If that's how it is, I've got to look at it."

If startled, Sharon might suck in her lip, hold it fast with her teeth.

"You turned it off because you couldn't face it, didn't you?"

"What are you saying? I couldn't face what?"

As plain as gospel, Sharon understood this as an accusation. What had she failed to look at? At the back of her eyes, where she couldn't avoid it, where, indeed, she had to confront it, she saw the iron frame of the bed, the sagging mattress evenly divided into two compartments, as if invisible bodies lay there, beneath the bed the gleaming, lidless night pot, and above it the dangling cord to the shadeless bulb. "It's not so hard to turn it off," Caroline said. "What's hard is to admit it." In her voice, in her gaze, Sharon felt Cora's inflexible will. Were they so much alike? Just in time, she cried out, "Watch the road!"

One wheel had edged into the ditch grass, sweeping the weeds. The car zigzagged wildly, the tires screeching, toppling the children about like pillows. They shrieked with pleasure. Perspiration filmed Sharon's face and throat; her lips and mouth were dry.

"Just think of it!" Caroline said, gripping the wheel as if to shake it. "The two of them together, sleeping and eating together, year in and year out, getting to loathe each other, none of it for the better, all of it for the worse—"

Sharon cried out, "Do you hear what you are saying?"

"They see it better than we do!" Caroline replied, but that was not Sharon's complaint. She was thinking of Cora, not the bug-eyed children, all ears, at her back. It seemed so obvious that Cora would hear, wherever she was, a voice as loud and brash as Caroline's. At a turn of the road the wind blew hotly into her face. If she kept her eyes closed, would it all fade away—what she had managed to face, and what she had preferred not to? Hearing grass sweep the bottom of the car, she opened her eyes. Caroline had driven off the road into a shallow ditch of high yellow weeds. Grasshoppers leaped to fall with a metallic click on the hood and the windshield. She remembered how Madge—Sharon had lacked the nerve—would hold the creatures firmly between her fingers and watch them spit "tobacco juice" like Emerson. The hardness of their bodies repelled Sharon. She would run screaming if they touched her. The sight of a sand viper wriggling through the grass would drain her face of blood, leave her speechless. Madge would take her by the arms and shake her. How explain such squeamishness in a country-born child?

Beyond the tall weeds that edged the road, tree stumps torn out by their roots were heaped at the center of a clearing. The deep pits left in the earth had not been filled. It brought to her mind the craters left by bombs. To the rear, almost the color of fire, ripe grain concealed the horizon, and far, far back, the blades of a harvester caught the light. Why had they stopped?

Matter-of-factly, Caroline said, "That's what's left." Sharon continued to gaze with light-creased eyes, a buzzing in her head. Even as she turned to look at Caroline she understood. This pitted field of the stumps of dead trees was all that was left of Cora's farm. All that was left of the trees, planted by Orion and Emerson, that had led all the way to the pasture, where Sharon and Madge, bringing in the cows, ran like the wind to keep from stepping on something. "Nobody wanted it," said Caroline. "There was nothing worth saving. When they get the stumps burned, Bryan'll plant it in soybeans. See there?" Sharon looked to where she pointed. A mixed patch of weeds, grain, and tall corn, including several hollyhocks, formed a small island. "That's where the barns sat, and the manure."

Sharon continued to stare, her tongue between her dry lips, pondering the imponderable. Into thin air. How did one measure air?

"I told Madge you could drive right by and not miss it." Did she feel any loss? Was it the emptiness that evoked the presence of Cora? Not her image, not her person, but the great alarming silence of her nature, the void behind her luminous eyes. It had frightened Sharon. Had she sensed a similar hollow in her own being? Cora Atkins had been for silence, and she would not have countenanced impertinent questions.

When she felt the deep silence of her soul threatened she had struck out with her hairbrush. All those unanswered questions were now asked of Sharon.

The car moved away slowly, crunching the gravel. A machine, almost as large as a house, came slowly toward them through a field of grain. Blades wheeled as if it might fly. It cut a swath through the field that left nothing but stubble. A dark pane of tinted glass concealed the driver, if it had one. Such a monster need only keep moving to level houses, barns, trees, anything in its path.

"Poor Cora!" Sharon blurted.

"I'll never forgive her," said Caroline. "Never."

"Caroline!" Sharon cried. She almost barked it, but her eagerness to hear more shamed her.

"She never complained. An animal would have complained. She would still be in all that rubble if they hadn't moved her."

A hand to her eyes, Sharon felt her head was splitting. The air trapped about her face smelled of flint.

"At least I can complain," Caroline said. "She couldn't."

With an effort, Sharon said, "She *could* have, Caroline, but she simply *wouldn't.*"

"Could or wouldn't, she didn't," said Caroline, "and now she's dead."

Once at the edge of town, within sight of the open fields, Ned and Madge Kibbee's house now backed up to an alley of commercial buildings that faced another street. Sharon would not have recognized it. The clapboards had been covered with green asbestos shingles to the height of the windows. A glassed-in porch the width of the house, with a metal awning to shade the doorway, had been added to the rear. In the side yard the stump of a tree was mounted with a teeter-totter. A larger and newer house loomed on the west, the shades drawn at the upper windows. The whine of a power machine, in a shop on the alley, rose to a siren pitch, then subsided.

"Daddy's retired," said Caroline, "but don't bring it up." She removed a bag of groceries from the car, then walked ahead of Sharon to the rear flight of steps. A pair of men's shoes, caked with grime and sawdust, sat left of the stoop. "Mom's probably in her bedroom, where it's cooler," Caroline said, but Madge was not in her bedroom. She heaved up from a couch covered with a sheet, and steadied herself by gripping the back of a chair. A summer-type frock, with a bright luau pattern, covered her like a hastily wrapped parcel. In her broad fleshy face the features had diminished, the eyes receded. A tremor was visible in the lenses of her glasses. As Sharon approached, she saw that Madge's eyes brimmed with tears.

"Why, she's pretty as ever!" Madge said to Caroline, her voice so firm it startled Sharon.

"I'm an old lady," Sharon replied.

"But you're a *little* old lady!" Her shoulders heaved. She might have been sobbing. She drew her hand from the back of the chair to cover her eyes. This show of emotion was relieved by Caroline.

"Where's Daddy?" she asked.

"He's napping. When it's so hot he don't sleep at night." A shadow stretched on the floor between them. Madge said, "Blanche, this is your Aunt Sharon. Sharon, you remember Blanche?"

Blanche stood framed in the kitchen doorway, the light outlining her wraith-like figure. Seeing Sharon, she crossed her arms so that her hands gripped her shoulders. In shyness a child might have done that, hugging herself in embarrassment. The light glowed in her thinning hair, outlining her skull.

"Of course I remember Blanche," Sharon said firmly. Owl-eyed, mute, she returned Sharon's gaze. What appeared to be jewels proved to be suds drying on her fingers. Unmistakably, she had Cora's lustrous eyes.

"She'd like to freshen up," said Madge. "Blanche, you get her a clean towel. She can lie down in your room if she wants to." She reached to touch Sharon's arm, gently. "You go along now. It's an hour before Bryan and Eileen get here. Fayrene and her girls will talk you silly. You better rest up."

Sharon followed the mute Blanche into and out of the kitchen, where pots steamed, through the dining room, blocked by the table and chairs, a card table stacked with silver, cups and saucers. From a room at the front, moving so quickly it seemed furtive, a figure slipped past them into the kitchen. Blanche gave no sign that she had seen it. Behind them, from the porch, Madge cried, "Ned, did you see her? Why, she's pretty as ever!" Did he reply? Sharon heard nothing. Blanche had preceded her into a bathroom, with room for little more than one person. She took both soiled towels from the rack with a quick, practiced gesture. A clean towel, thin as the curtain at the window, she placed on the rim of the washbowl. On the sill of the window there were bottles containing seeds, leaves, and creatures feeding on them.

"Thank you," Sharon said.

Blanche replied, "You're welcome," as if Sharon had thanked her for cleaning the erasers. Flies hovered in the dim light of the hall, making no noise. Blanche went ahead of her into the room at the front, where she puffed up the pillow, drew the blind at the window. Again Sharon said, "Thank you." Again she replied, "You're welcome." She left the room with her eyes averted, not glancing back.

No one, of course, had written Sharon to say that Ned Kibbee had not *prospered.* They would never say failed, but they might acknowledge he hadn't prospered. The assured and capable young man Madge had married, a builder of houses, would never grow to be the silent, stooped old man who had slithered past her, furtive as a rabbit. What had happened? Sharon turned on her side, lifting a corner of the blind, as if she might see. Down the street, where the trees thinned, were new houses. Here and there sprinklers were running. New cars were parked along the curbs. A TV flickered on a screened-in porch. Lying back,

Sharon gazed at the wall at the foot of her bed. Heat-drugged flies hovered near the light cord. In the blind-filtered light she could dimly see figures on the faded wallpaper, drawn with thin white lines, as on a blue-print. The pattern was flat, without perspective, but objects in the foreground were larger. In the wall of a house the windows were unevenly spaced. The door appeared to be centered, but lacked steps to reach the ground. Much smaller in size was a barn, with the door open to the hayloft. A small figure sat there. Trees, like stalks of celery, thrust up to one side. To the right of the house a stick-thin figure, wearing a stocking cap, held a pail. Of her stay with Sharon Rose, of Briarcliffe, of Chicago, an exotic-looking bird, with a dishevelled topknot, was perched on one of the leaf fronds in the wallpaper. The eyes were open, and bright as hatpins. The wall was streaked with color smears and erasures.

It calmed Sharon to lie quiet on the bed, puzzling it out. Its outline so pale Sharon had overlooked it, a mailbox, on a post, was propped up in a milk can. This object startled her. She had always found it too high to reach. Orion would sometimes lift her from the ground and hold her while she pulled down the lid and peered in. There was seldom mail, but often newspapers and circulars. Orion would then lower her to the ground and she would run with the mail to Cora. But she had lost interest when she could do all this by herself.

Once she had a beau Madge was always the first to

look for the mail. When Lillian wrote to Sharon, Madge would bring her the letter, then wait for the stamp. Sharon was very much concerned what Ned wrote to Madge, but all Madge seemed concerned about were the stamps. Sharon did not understand her. Didn't she see what was happening? In many of her letters Lillian would enclose a small gift, perhaps a handkerchief from Marshall Field & Co. in Chicago, which Madge cared nothing about, but Sharon could sense that it troubled Cora. If it had not been for Lillian, what might her life have been like? She fell into a reverie, both pleasurable and troubling, involving the child-like drawings on the wall and the complexity of her emotions. Were the drawings recent? An effort to recover what had disappeared? On the front side of the house, with its oddly spaced windows, was a door that lacked steps down to the yard. As a child, barely able to walk, Sharon had fallen from the sill into matted grass, and from that moment, to her knowledge, the screen had been kept latched. The door itself stood open to air out the house, but was never used to enter or exit. Drawn in, then erased from the scene, was a tree that had died after Fayrene's marriage. Had it posed a problem? Did it belong among those things that were beyond recovery?

At the door a voice said, "Aunt Sharon, you awake?"

She considered a moment, but remained silent. The voice did not return. Later she pushed up, as if she might cry out, to see a ghostly figure in the bureau mirror, the hair disheveled, one side of the face wind-burned, putting her in mind of a piece of iron-scorched lace. Then she slept. Not till evening, hearing the clatter of dishes, did she wake up.

Three leaves had been added to the dining room table to accommodate the grownups. The children, Crystal, Carl, and Ardene, sat at a card table between the folding doors. As at her first meeting with Avery Dickel, Sharon faced him across the table, a hulking, graying man who sat waiting for his food, gripping his knife and fork. The gross features, so loutish in a youth, were almost handsome in the ripened man, but a snow of dandruff sprinkled the lapels of his coat. Did he remember her rudeness? He had stooped to scoop up the cat Moses, mewing for food, to curl back the lips and scrape the tartar from its yellow teeth with his thumbnail. The mere memory of it caused her to shudder. Was that one more of the many things she preferred not to face? Caroline sat on his right, and her glance suggested that in one form or another she had heard the story, and that in her opinion animals were better judges of character than some people. Eileen, seated on Avery's left, had a touch of red in her hair and the freckles believed to be from Avery's side of the family. She sat erect, her figure spare as Cora's, her lips firm over teeth that needed adjusting. At her side, Bryan tilted back on his chair to keep his gaze on the light at the window. His left arm rested on the back of Eileen's chair, his finger toying with the collar of her blouse. She gave no sign that this pleased or displeased her.

Maureen Dickel, almost as tall as her father, sat

slouched on the piano stool at Sharon's left. She had Avery's hands and large-boned wrists, around which she absently twisted her napkin. To put her more at ease, Sharon asked her what she planned to do. In a reply so casual Sharon was hardly attentive, Maureen said that whatever she did she planned to live life to the full. It left Sharon too surprised to ask what the fullness of this life might include. In a shrill voice, Crystal, who had heard Sharon's question, shrieked that Maureen worked for Dr. Lewin, and they all went to her to have their teeth cleaned.

"Shut your trap," Maureen replied.

"If there's not employment here, there is in O'Neill or Sydney," said Madge.

"There is if you're a woman," said Ned. These were the first words he had spoken, but Sharon sensed that they had heard them many times.

Avery raised his head as if he would speak, but seeing Sharon, he thought better of it. Time had not altered his open-mouthed, unconscious gaze. Caroline said that those who were willing to work no longer had to go somewhere else to do it, if they had a trade. Eileen said that farmers didn't lack for work, if it was farming, but the way things were going, not many could afford to. It cost Bryan four hundred dollars more a month to farm than the farm paid. They had heard that before too, but they knew that Sharon hadn't, and allowed time for it to sink in.

"I'm afraid I don't understand," she replied.

Bryan tilted forward to rest his arms on the table. He raised a fork to wag it in Sharon's direction.

"There's nothing much to understand, ma'am," he said. "It costs me four dollars a bushel to grow wheat they sell to the Russians for a dollar thirty."

Eileen said, "Which was why Bryan switched to soybeans."

"But I'm still losing money. I've got farm machinery that cost me double what we paid for the house."

Caroline said he couldn't blame on the Russians what was the fault of the commodities market.

Shit on the commodities market, he replied. They sat silent, as if waiting for grace. "The thing I liked about Vietnam," Bryan said, "was that over there at least I knew who to shoot at. Now that I'm back here I'm no longer so sure who the enemy is."

Was it their custom to ignore him? Blanche came from the kitchen with a basket of rolls, a plate of celery, radishes, and olives. Bryan was the first to help himself to the olives. Blanche said, "Fayrene, you want to see that Sharon gets some of the pickle relish. It's part of Cora's last batch."

The glass extended toward Sharon, its peeling paper label bearing the words "P. Relish" in Cora's crabbed hand, was of a watery blue color and had originally been used for jelly. These glasses had been stored at the back of the storm cave, and once required both of Sharon's small hands to lift one. The back side of the seal of wax had a syrup of jelly she was allowed to lick off. To no avail, Cora tirelessly cautioned Emerson not to spoon jelly with the spoon he had just licked off. "I'm going to lick it off later," he would reply, as if that settled the matter.

"Just smell it!" said Fayrene, the one thing Sharon was reluctant to do. The acrid smell of the relish prepared in Cora's steaming kitchen had often pursed Sharon's lips like the taste of lemon. Fayrene used a fork to serve her a portion, but Sharon was reluctant to taste it. The words "blood of my blood, flesh of my flesh" came to her lips as if spoken.

Madge said, "I don't know what I'd do without Blanche," as Blanche stooped to serve Ned some peas in a cream sauce.

Ned said, "I like canned peas better than fresh ones, always did."

The smear of flour on Blanche's cheek was less white than her flawless complexion. Was she never in the sun? Madge brushed the flour from her cheek with a flick of her napkin. Behind her closed lips she nibbled on something, but her mind (her *mind?*) was elsewhere. She did not feel the focus of Sharon's gaze. The plate of celery and olives that Avery was hoarding she took from him to extend toward Sharon. In the exchange of glances Sharon remarked only the long twisted lashes.

Fayrene excused herself to rise from the table and fasten napkins to the fronts of the children. The men settled down to eating, their heads lowered over their plates. Sharon had been hungry when she sat down, but the oven fumes on the draft from the kitchen, the sight of mouths chewing, the platter of fried chicken with the side bowl of pan gravy, made her slightly nauseous. The disturbance was physical, one of displacement, with objects and persons in the wrong places, at the wrong time. She was asked by Maureen if she liked to fly, which did not help. Her face filmed with perspiration, chewing slowly, Madge sat in a digestive reverie, her eyes upward, scanning the ceiling. She flicked her napkin at flies that settled on the food. Blanche kept their glasses full of iced tea, and Fayrene helped her clear the dishes from the table. Homemade strawberry ice cream, hand cranked by Ned (the only thing not the same being the frozen strawberries), was served from a bowl that cooled Sharon like a cake of ice as she held it. Avery scooped the ice cream to his mouth, chewed and swallowed it like mashed potatoes. Ned said, "You know how you know when it's real ice cream? It hurts your teeth." There was a murmur of assent, but Madge shook her head. Time was allowed for the cream she had in her mouth to melt. "You know it's real ice cream," she said, "when it waxes the roof of your mouth."

For the time it took Sharon to place a napkin to her lips, her head nodding in agreement, all those seated around the table were animated by a common, agreeable emotion. They smiled with their eyes. Avery Dickel pushed back his chair, as if to speak. In the pause, while they waited, insects could be heard buzzing at the screen. This sound moved Sharon in a way that filmed her eyes. Across from her, Avery Dickel had tilted back his head to observe something on or near the ceiling. Sharon was not able to see it, but what she heard was like the fluttering of a moth trapped under the shade of a lamp or behind a blind. Bryan, tilted back on his chair, sat with an amused smile on his lips. The sound increased to where it seemed to hover directly over Sharon's head. A fine powdering of dust and bits of feather fell on her face when she glanced upward.

"That's where Blanche usually sits," said Madge. "She thinks it's Blanche."

The bird, a parakeet or a canary, hovered as if it intended to nest in Sharon's hair. Did she gasp? The startled bird rose toward the ceiling, then in a faltering, bobbing flight it moved from head to head, circling the table, pausing as if confused over the head of Caroline.

"Blanche!" she cried, waving her napkin at the bird.

Hearing her name, Blanche came to the door of the kitchen, the apron and its loose strings dangling at her front. In one hand she held a wooden spoon filmed with the ice cream she had been licking. The charm of this picture, the child-woman framed in the door to the cluttered kitchen, held their attention as if they waited for her to speak. Madge said, "Show Sharon how she gives you a kiss," and as Blanche extended her hand, the bird fluttered to perch on her finger. Her eyes wide with delight, she brought the chirping bird close to her face, her lips wide in a frozen "cheese" expression, as the bird chirped and eagerly pecked at the particles of food between her teeth. Carl and Crystal giggled nervously. Avery Dickel said, "It probably thinks it's eating corn on the cob." He guffawed, then fell silent. Sharon could hear the sharp metallic click of the beak on the teeth. She believed her eyes, but her emotions were confounded. The kinship seemed so natural Sharon would not have been surprised if the bird had picked lice out of her hair. She felt withdrawn from the scene, as if she saw it through a window, or within the frame of a painting. In something she had read, so long ago it seemed a memory, a bird had flown into a hall crowded with warriors, in a window at one end and out at the other, leading one of them to observe that its brief flight, out of darkness and back into darkness, was like life itself.

Caroline startled them all by sharply clapping her hands. The sound, of course, frightened the bird, which rose to flutter wildly for a moment on the ceiling, until Blanche moved to where she could raise her hand and provide it a perch. She stroked its soiled, balding head with one finger as she walked from the room. Sharon glanced—no more, just a quick, passing glance—to see that Caroline sat with her eyes lowered, as if in thought. She had been fearless in revealing what had been concealed, in resolutely confronting what had been hidden, but the most appalling facts were those that burned like gems in the open. Not in the bedroom only, or in the barn, or in the mind's dim recesses, but in the shimmering light that rose from the fields and buzzed with the drone of insects. On the palm of her hand Sharon felt again the stinging slap of Cora's brush. No matter how fearlessly youthful eyes stared, or youthful voices cried out what should not be mentioned, the tongue would prove to be silent, the eyes lidded, in matters that were secret to the heart. In that way—how else?—it was possible to guess at what they were.

"Just because she don't talk," said Madge, "don't think she misses out on much, for she don't."

In the kitchen they could hear the bird chirping. Fayrene rose from the table to slap the hands of Crystal, who was using her fingers to fish the mini-marshmallows out of the fruit salad. Lips parted, Crystal mimicked Blanche's frozen "cheese" smile. "Don't you make a face at me!" Fayrene said, and gave her a slap. It brought a fiery glow to Crystal's freckled cheek and closed her mouth, but not her bright button eyes. Whatever she saw, would she see it, like Sharon, for the rest of her life?

They drove to Cora's service, in Battle Creek, in Avery's new station wagon, the cushions already strewn with dog fur. They passed under the tree from which Sharon had once been swept from the back of a horse. Madge did not exchange glances with her. Ned Kibbee, seated on her left, appeared to sleep. In the funeral hall Blanche sat beside her father, her hands in her lap, her wide-eyed serene gaze on the window that opened on the schoolyard, where children were playing. Their voices distracted Sharon from the service, but part of her mind listened to the music. *Abide with me.* She pondered the meaning of the words. But what, indeed, had abided? The liberation from her burdens, the works and meager effects of Cora had been erased from the earth. If she had guessed, Sharon would have felt her speechless humiliation. Others could, and would, grasp it painlessly as a metaphor. Cora would not have grasped it. The violation, like a shaking of the earth, was too profound. Her death was an incident of small importance compared with this ultimate rejection. Works and days. Her soul had made its peace with things. The comb she had pulled through Sharon's tangled hair, more than half the teeth missing, had been placed on the bureau. If questioned, Cora would have replied that since she had lost more than half of her hair, they were well matched.

The half-submerged life had stifled Sharon, and she had fled. Vivid as the tableaus in the museum in Lincoln, of early man and extinct monsters, she saw herself in the plush-covered train seat on her way to Chicago, and freedom. In the aisle at her back, clutching his fiber laundry carton, a young man leaned forward to rub a clear spot in the window with the heel of his hand. But the smear of grime proved to be on the outside, not the in. "It's up ahead," he had said. "What is?" she asked. In the window she saw his reflection, his eyes moving as he searched the darkness. "Boy, am I glad to see the last of that!" he had exclaimed. A lifetime later, his ignorance, his great expectations, brought a film to Sharon's eyes, an ache to her throat. Had he led his own life, as she had, only to find that it led back to where he had started, his eyes fastened on the darkness where he hoped to see a glimpse of familiar light? Had they both grown up and old in order to recover what had escaped them as children? In the aisles of a supermarket, in Boston, Sharon had heard one young woman say to another, "I'm now seriously into music." *Into* music. Had

Sharon winced at the triteness of the phrase, or at its truth? Where else had she been but into music? There had been a moment, yes, there *had* been a moment, when she might have seriously got into something else, but the pain of an early rejection had seemed stronger than a future attraction. As much as or more than the child she had borne, Sharon had been Cora's girl. Abstinence was something she understood; indulgence she did not.

At the door to the chapel Caroline said, more in admiration than in anger, "If anybody ever earned a rest, she did." One of the many facts of life she had trained herself to face.

Late in the afternoon, Bryan drove Sharon and Blanche to Grand Island in his new pickup, a truck so high off the road it frightened Sharon to look out the window. Blanche had come along with them just for the ride. Eileen had explained that of all things, including the movies, she liked to ride around in the pickup the most. An FM radio played rock music. The air conditioner blew a chill draft on Sharon's legs. Now and then Bryan helped himself to a butterscotch lozenge from the pack on the dashboard. As the twilight deepened, the bowl of the sky glowed with an ethereal light. Sharon's face, reflected in the window, was like that of an old worn coin. On the darkening plain her eyes searched for lights in the farmhouse windows. A sweet sadness, a longing touched with dread, filled her with a tender, pleasurable self-pity. Whatever life held in the future for her, it would prove to reside in this rimless past, approaching and then fading like the gong of a crossing bell. In Blanche's muteness, in her elusive presence, Sharon felt their mutual kinship with the child buried in the grave without a marker, nameless as the flowers pressed between the pages of Cora's Bible. Houses and barns, the living and the dead, into thin air. In the cab of the pickup, the blacktop flowing soundlessly beneath them, Sharon was at once incredulous and believing, at one with the world and fearlessly detached. Did the young orbiting in space feel a similar bafflement and elevation?

The monotonous swirling and beat of the music confused and drowsed her senses. She fitfully dozed. At a three-way intersection of streaming traffic she awoke. Beyond the stoplights, a huge sign advertised the Crossways Inn. A pattern of moving lights traced the outline of an Indian shooting an arrow at the sky. In the space reserved for messages she read that WOMEN WORLD WIDE were in assembly, and that children under 12, accompanied by their parents, were free.

"Is that possible?" she asked.

Bryan did not seem to hear her. He drove the pickup under the shelter at the entrance, then walked around the car to help her down from the cab. Blanche appeared to be seated back from the window in a darkened room. Sharon called to her, wagging her fingers, then followed Bryan into the bustling throng of the air-cooled lobby. Young and matronly women, many of them wearing blue jackets with large name labels, moved about with professional assurance. There were few men. A large poster with a likeness of Alexandra Selkirk was partially covered with petitions to sign and graffiti. At intervals bells rang. Bryan left her side to inquire at the desk about her reservation. He was given a key, which he brought back to Sharon. He did not conceal how ill at ease he felt in a swarm of women.

"It was good to see and talk to you, ma'am," he said. "It did Eileen a lot of good."

"I do hope everything works out."

"It always does," he replied. "It just don't work out the way you want it."

He was at once flattering and patronizing. She was an old and frail woman, but substantial enough to deserve his frankness. She was relieved he didn't offer to escort her to her room. Here in the lobby of the Crossways Inn she breathed the bracing air of womanly independence. A young woman with a clipboard approached Sharon, said, "If you'll excuse me," and looked at the number on her room key. "That's to your left," she said. "Follow the arrows toward the swimming pool."

Sharon moved in that direction, but she was stopped by a blast of applause and appreciative howls that came from a dark, grotto-like entrance. Back in the cave-like gloom a blue light focused on a bizarre figure. The light emphasized his corpse-like pallor. He —or was it she?—sat on a stool, one knee drawn up to the chest, the other long limb twined around the stool leg. The tails of a denim shirt draped the stool seat. Drab olive-green pants, with bulging thigh pockets, were wrapped about his calves like leggings. The gaunt face was solemn. Reddish hair grew up from his head as if sucked by a fan. Sharon thought of a gargoyle. A chill prickled the flesh of her arms. From the dark at his side he raised a guitar, lowered his head to the strings so that he looked like a hunchback. Pretending to pluck the strings delicately, he mimed the words of an obscene song. Sharon was spellbound. Her flesh crawled, an expression she had always found ridiculous. His crouching, cringing manner, the subtle movement of his fingers, conveyed as words could not the corruption of his nature. She stared, her eyes wide, her lips parted, powerless to move or to resist his suggestions. At the crotch of his legs, thrusting upward and outward, the black shaft of the microphone, nudged by his knee, wagged like a tailpiece. Was she hypnotized? She knew that she was watching a simulated orgasm. His body jerked convulsively. An explosion of applause and hooting indicated the performance was over. She saw only the top of his bowed head, like a tangled string mop.

"Why don't I just show you," said the same young woman (Sharon noted that her name was Deborah). She took the key from her hand and proceeded down the corridor to the left. At points where the halls intersected, illuminated arrows indicated the rooms. Sharon's proved to be near the swimming pool, the ceiling of the corridor rippling with the reflections off the water. On the knob of the door a card had been turned to read DO NOT DISTURB. The room was not occupied, however, but proved to be full of the previous occupant's smoke. The color TV was on, sound-less but alive with animated faces.

"You come from far?" Deborah asked. Sharon paused to consider. "I'm from Salem, near Portland. The two girls next to you"—she pointed—"are from Atlanta. We're from all over, not just from the dust bowl." At the door she said, "Leave your valuables at the desk. Keep the door locked."

Sharon thanked her. On the TV smoke was rising from a forest fire, planes were diving. Behind the drapes at the window she could hear the cries of children in the swimming pool.

The life congenial to Sharon, however melancholy, is the world of phantoms, more alluring than dreams, that impinges on her dreaming. The pervasive tone is a sweet sadness, a pleasurable longing, suffused with drug-like strains of music. Longing for what? Signs are visible. A child is sometimes seen wearing a blindfold, groping about as if for companions. A voice says, "It is not your longing, but part of the world's longing." A profound recognition sweetens her sorrow. She moves, she floats, she glides, she gasps to see the earth receding behind her, space unfolding before her. Bells are ringing. It proves to be the phone beside the bed.

"You didn't call." It was Alexandra Selkirk. Her voice was hoarse.

"I fell asleep." In the mirror Sharon saw that she was fully clothed, except for her shoes.

"I can't imagine how. It's a bedlam. Shall we eat in my room?" At the thought of food Sharon was silent. "I don't hear you."

"How did it go?" Sharon asked.

"Darling, I wowed 'em. But I am famished. The number is one-nine-four. The door will be open. I'll be in the tub."

Sharon asked, "What time is it?"

"Twenty minutes past one." Sharon was silent. "One-nine-four," said Alexandra. "The door is open." She hung up.

Swimmers could be heard bouncing the diving board, splashing in the pool. An amorous couple, the woman in pajamas, stood grappling in the warmth of the laundry room, like a single two-headed monster. They pressed against a cart full of billowing soiled sheets. Just one day before Sharon would not have marveled at the forces that brought such loose ends together, making them one. At intervals bells rang, flashing lights seemed to beckon. Here and there doors stood open, TVs flickered through clouds of smoke. Dishes were piled on carts, trays of bottles and glasses in which the ice still melted lined the corridor walls. At the intersection of two hallways, a man and a woman sat on the stairs, the woman sobbing. Her head rested on his shoulder, as he patted her arm. Sharon saw that her clasped hands were trembling. "Can I help?" she asked.

The woman shuddered like a cold child. It moved Sharon to take a step closer. The man said, "You got any Valium? She's off it. She's got the withdrawals." Hearing these words, the woman whimpered.

"What can I do?" Sharon pleaded.

"Ma'am," he replied, in a gentle voice, "what can we do to be saved?"

This astonishing statement startled Sharon, like a sign of life in something believed dead. Much that had happened on this endless day relieved her of a burden she had long carried, but had been reluctant to acknowledge. The woman continued to tremble, whimpering softly, pressing her clasped hands to her front.

Sharon moved away, wandering aimlessly, erect and serene as a sleepwalker. Without searching she found room 194, the door slightly ajar. Alexandra, in a white terry robe, stood in the archway at the back, toweling her hair. The light was such that the veins of her arms, drained of blood, were like the grain in wood. A memory Sharon had obliterated flooded her mind. Through the floor ventilator in the upstairs hall she had once spied on Cora bathing herself in a washtub. Her lean body had been folded to fit the space, her arms and shoulders were lathered with soap. One hand, holding a jelly glass, scooped water from the space between her knees to pour it over her head. Sharon was all eyes. Never before had she seen a grown-up person without clothes. Was she a crawling baby, or a growing child who had left her bed to witness this ceremony? It was a single image out of time, but rooted in place, stored unseen and unacknowledged till the moment the door opened on Alexandra. On the instant, involuntary, Sharon was being fitted for new clothes by Cora, who stood behind her, the silence broken by the crinkle of the pattern paper. She held pins between her lips. She would not speak until she had used them up. Accompanying this sound and image there was also the smell of the hot iron, and the scorched board pad.

Her arms lowered and dangling, her short hair tousled, Alexandra resembled an exotic, stork-legged bird. She said, "Who said let there be light? *He* did. Who saw that all of it was good? *He* did. Who said let us make him in our image? *He* did. Who said let them have dominion over the whole shebang. *He* did. We've been living under him all of these goddamn centuries. When I swear, 'My God!' what am I doing, Sharon Rose, tell me that?"

In spite of what she heard, of what was said, Sharon was comforted. When she heard the voice of Alexandra she heard *his* voice, and knew she was in good hands. That was her feeling, of course: the uppermost of the feelings she was able to bear.

A rhythmic thumping pounded the floor directly overhead. Alexandra dropped the towel she was holding to reach for a cigarette, light it, inhale it. As she exhaled the smoke, the thumping returned.

"Why don't I call the desk?" Sharon asked, and called it. The buzzer sounded, but no answer. Voices passed in the hall, singing. Alexandra parted the drapes at the rear and peered into the court. The light that streamed in was like that at an airport. Once more Sharon dialed the desk.

"Yes?"

"There is a loud thumping in the ceiling. We can't sleep. Something must be done about it."

The voice at the desk was not surprised. "Let me see if I can figure out who's above you. I'll call you back."

Sharon thanked her, said to Alexandra, "She's going to call us back."

Alexandra said, "I will never know this person, but I hate him. If I had a gun, I would shoot him. There should be more crimes of this type."

The phone rang. The voice said, "What you're hearing, ma'am, is someone practicing on a drum."

"You're asking me to believe someone is beating a drum?"

"Yes, ma'am. It's the Oneida Marching Band in the rooms above you."

"It's going to stop?"

"Oh, I wouldn't say that. They need the practice. Hold on a minute, will you?" Sharon held on. "I'm back," she said. "I guess they put you in the wrong wing. Nobody expects to sleep in that wing."

Sharon said, "This is the room of Alexandra Selkirk, the distinguished speaker at the convention. Can we have another room?"

"There's no more rooms, ma'am."

"Let me speak to the manager," said Sharon.

"Oh, he won't be here until eight o'clock."

Sharon was not equal to this occasion. She looked for help to Alexandra, who stood smoking with her eyes closed. There was someone at the door. The food Alexandra ordered, covered with gleaming hot lids, was pushed in on a cart. The young woman was huge, with a round, childish face, the body of a circus fat lady. She beamed at Sharon with good humor. Packets of sugar, saccharin, and a dairy substitute were in a plastic glass. Alexandra poured coffee from the thermos into a cup, added three packets of sugar, slurped a mouthful.

"My God, it's coffee."

"Fresh made," said the young woman. "I just made it."

Alexandra appeared to see her for the first time. "Are you married?" she asked.

Her head pumped. "We just bought a house in Kearney, near the Greyhound station. He drives a bus. I work nights, he works days for Greyhound. He says what we need a house for since we're seldom in it?"

"What do you need it for?"

"Tax deductions. With two salaries, we pay a lot of taxes."

Alexandra held the cup of coffee with both hands, as if to warm her fingers, steam her face.

"Is that all, ma'am?"

That was all. As the door closed behind her, Alexandra said, "If I had had a child it would have been like that one." Sharon wondered in what way she meant it. The gulps of hot coffee seemed to have roused her. "We've got the energy," she said, her voice rising.

"We've got an atomic bomb right here in this building. Just the energy in this madhouse, you hear me, would put a rocket in space, light up a city!" She raised one hand before her, invoking silence. "And don't tell me it's not *our* energy," she cried, "more than it is *his!*"

Seated on the bed, Sharon watched Alexandra eat a slice of rare prime rib, ignoring the vegetables. Each bite, it seemed to Sharon, was visibly transformed into energy. Her short hair stood on end. "How was your day?" she asked, buttering a roll.

Of the six days of creation, which one had it been? Alexandra waited for Sharon to speak. "In the hall just now"—Alexandra sipped her coffee; was she listening?—"I was asked what we should do to be saved." Speaking these words brought a smile of recognition to Sharon's lips. Alexandra was silent. There was a pause while she filled Sharon's cup with coffee. "Was it a man or a woman?" she asked.

"Both, I think," Sharon replied, as feelings with which she did not pretend to cope rose in her like a fever. She sipped the coffee. Through the film on her eyes the objects in the room appeared to melt.

Alexandra said, "Do you suppose it's the sugar? I feel better." She walked to open the drapes at the patio doors. Someone was swimming laps in the pool. Above the flash of the signs the sky was black. "Did you hear that?" she asked. At some distance a young rooster brazenly crowed. The sound was piercing, but cracked, shrill with young male assurance, transporting Sharon to the hush of a summer dawn, the faint stain of light between the sill and the blind at her window, the house dark as a cave, in the stairwell the sounds of stove lids being lifted, shifted, the pungent whiff of kerosene spilled on the cobs, the rasp of a match, and in the silence following the whoosh and roar of the flames the first clucking of the hens in the henhouse, all of it gone, vanished from this earth, but restored to the glow of life in a cock's crow.

"You hear that?" said Alexandra. "The same old tyrant!" Was it a smile she turned to share with Sharon or a grimace? This would be a young tyrant, not an old one, but it seemed unimportant in the context. His voice gained in assurance as the thumping in the ceiling subsided.

"It just occurred to me it's Sunday," Alexandra said, and looked around for her slippers. From a hanger on the door she took her cloak and let it drape loosely about her shoulders. The nightgown beneath it might have been a party frock. Against the light of the bathroom her flat, skeletal figure appeared to be a resurrection of Cora. She faced the mirror to draw a comb through her short coarse hair. As if hallucinating, Sharon seemed to see a wire-handled syrup pail dangling from her hand, weighted with eggs. Glass eggs weighted the pockets of one of Emerson's sweaters.

Still facing the mirror, Alexandra said, "I'm going for a walk. I want to see the sunrise. Do you know the sun is perpetually rising? Every moment somewhere. Isn't that awesome?" What she saw in the mirror led her to smile. She turned to say, "You want to join me?"

What expression did she surprise on Sharon's face?

For a moment it shamed her, it was so open, betraying her customary independence.

Alexandra said, "Do I look a sight? Who is there to see me but God?"

Sharon had already moved to rise from the bed. "I'm coming," she said. "I've not seen a sunrise since I was a child."

Nonpareil Books

FICTION

Reuben Bercovitch
Hasen
160 pages, $8.95

José Donoso
The Obscene Bird of Night
448 pages, $12.95

Stanley Elkin
The Franchiser
360 pages, $10.95

Searches & Seizures
320 pages, $10.95

Marian Engel
Bear
144 pages, $9.95

Paula Fox
Desperate Characters
176 pages, $9.95

William H. Gass
In the Heart of the Heart of the Country
340 pages, $10.95

Paul Horgan
A Distant Trumpet
628 pages, $16.95

Joy Kogawa
Obasan
250 pages, $11.95

William Maxwell
The Chateau
416 pages, $12.95

The Folded Leaf
288 pages, $11.95

The Old Man at the Railroad Crossing
192 pages, $10.95

Over by the River
256 pages, $10.95

Time Will Darken It
320 pages, $10.95

They Came Like Swallows
192 pages, $9.95

So Long, See You Tomorrow
174 pages, $9.95

Wright Morris
Collected Stories 1948-1986
274 pages, $10.95

Plains Song: For Female Voices
232 pages, $10.95

Howard Frank Mosher
Disappearances
272 pages, $10.95

Robert Musil
Five Women
224 pages, $10.95

Liam O'Flaherty
Famine
480 pages, $12.95

Mary Robison
An Amateur's Guide to the Night
144 pages, $9.95

Days
192 pages, $9.95

Oh!
224 pages, $9.95

Peter Rushforth
Kindergarten
208 pages, $10.95

Maurice Shadbolt
Season of the Jew
384 pages, $12.95

Among the Cinders
218 pages, $10.95

Nonpareil Books returns to print books acknowledged as classics. All *Nonpareils* are printed on acid-free paper and are produced to the highest standards. They are permanent softcover books designed for use and made to last. For a complete list, please write to David R. Godine, Publisher.

David R. Godine, Publisher
NONPAREIL BOOKS
300 Massachusetts Avenue
Boston, Massachusetts 02115